Jesus Is Victor!

Jesus Is Victor!

Karl Barth's Doctrine of Salvation

Donald G. Bloesch

Abingdon
Nashville

JESUS IS VICTOR! KARL BARTH'S DOCTRINE OF SALVATION

Copyright © 1976 by Abingdon

Library of Congress Cataloging in Publication Data

BLOESCH, DONALD G. 1928-
  Jesus is victor!
  Includes index.
  1. Salvation—History of doctrines. 2. Barth, Karl, 1886-1968. I.
Title.
BT751.2.B54   234   76-14360

ISBN 0-687-20225-6

MANUFACTURED BY THE PARTHENON PRESS AT
NASHVILLE, TENNESSEE, UNITED STATES OF AMERICA

To Mary Jackson,
my mother-in-law

If you have heard the Easter message, you can no longer run around with a tragic face and lead the humourless existence of a man who has no hope. One thing still holds, and only this one thing is really serious, that Jesus is the Victor.

And everything took place in this crucifixion—the whole reconciliation, the whole restoration of peace between man and God.

—Karl Barth

Contents

Foreword

I have been led to write this book partly in order to counteract popular misunderstandings of Karl Barth's theology and also partly to show how authentically modern Barth really is. To be sure, I have concentrated on his doctrine of salvation, but this is where much of the controversy has developed. It is also my purpose to demonstrate that Barth falls short of constructing a theology that is both fully evangelical and catholic, though he has made great strides toward it.

It is commonly thought that Barth is anti-cultural and even obscurantist, but this can be gleaned only from a cursory and superficial examination of his earlier works. For Barth the creative aspirations and accomplishments of man have their ultimate basis in the providential and redemptive grace of God, though culture itself is not redemptive nor is it a source of redemption. Indeed, it will be argued that Barth stands in the tradition of the Enlightenment as well as that of the Reformation.

Another criticism, one particularly prominent in conservative Protestant circles, is that Barth sees evil only in terms of privation and deficiency. These ideas are not absent in his thought, but the Nothingness or the Nihil, his term for the abyss of darkness or evil, indicates not simply a lack of goodness but something diabolical and abominable. It is not a mere omission of the good nor a preparation for the good (as in Schleiermacher) but its antithesis. It is that which God does not will and therefore that which is radically excluded from his creation. It is given a certain negative reality by virtue of the divine rejection, but it has only a provisional status in the plan of salvation. The objection that Barth does not see the devil as a personal adversary of God and man has some merit, but even here it should be pointed out that the Nothingness often assumes a personal mask in his theology.

My principal criticism of Barth's theology is that he ever and again fails to hold together the objective and subjective poles of salvation, and yet I must acknowledge that on occasion he does succeed in maintaining this delicate balance. While contending that everything needful for our salvation has been accomplished in Jesus Christ, he makes clear that this still has to be apprehended and appropriated by sinful man. The atonement is not only a divine act and offer but includes an active human participation in it. At the same time it cannot be denied that the emphasis in his theology is definitely on the objective side. Even in speaking of the subjective appropriation, Barth has in mind primarily Jesus Christ in his humanity and only secondarily those who are engrafted into Christ. A theological rationalism seems to take precedence over the dialectic theology, especially in his *Church Dogmatics* after Volume I. He can perhaps be accused of becoming more scholastic and less dialectical and paradoxical as his work proceeded.

One of the main questions I shall deal with is whether Barth's theology is in fact a "new modernism," as Van Til alleges,[1] or whether he stands in basic continuity with the faith of the Reformation. Is he actually a child of the Enlightenment or a son of Calvin and Luther? Or does he transcend the cleavage between the Reformation and the Enlightenment and effect a new synthesis, not one in which Christ is seen as the fulfillment of culture (as in Thomas Aquinas) but one that depicts him as the transformer of culture? I think it can be shown that Barth does move in this direction; at the same time it would be more proper to say that he points to an eschatological synthesis, since he insists that the transformation that occurs now is only partial.

It cannot be denied that Barth's overall diagnosis of the human situation is optimistic, perhaps too optimistic; and yet we must remember that his optimism is based on the incomparable victory of Christ, not the natural potentiality of man. He avers that in the light of Christ it becomes evident that all people are encompassed by God's grace, that all are claimed by his love. Yet apart from Christ man is lost and condemned, and apart from the Holy Spirit man can do nothing but evil. Bearing this in mind, we can

11

understand these words of Barth: "Man is not naturally disposed to hear the Word of God: we are children of wrath."[2]

I must admit that when I first began this project I was more averse to Barth's doctrine of salvation than when I ended. I became more positively disposed toward Barth as I continued my research, though I expect I shall never be a bona fide Barthian. His influence is definitely perceptible in many of my earlier writings. For some time his theological method has elicited my admiration and support. I have benefited greatly from his writings but have nevertheless always sought to maintain a critical stance, which may disconcert some thoroughgoing Barthians. In some areas of theology Barth has been an invaluable ally and in other areas a useful foil.

My denominational background is that branch within the Evangelical and Reformed church (now the United Church of Christ) which was formerly known as the Evangelical Synod; this body was more Lutheran than Calvinistic, more Pietistic than rationalistic or confessionalistic. Personal faith and piety were deemed nearly as important as God's reconciling act in Jesus Christ. This perhaps at least partially accounts for the problems that I have had with the Barthian theology as well as the fascination that it has exerted upon me.

I wish to acknowledge the help that I have received from Dr. G. W. Bromiley of Fuller Theological Seminary in understanding the nuances in certain German words that are especially pivotal in

Barth's doctrine of salvation. I also wish to thank the T. & T. Clark Publishing Company in Edinburgh, Scotland, for granting me permission for the many quotations from Karl Barth's *Church Dogmatics*. Finally I am deeply grateful to my wife, Brenda, for her helpful suggestions and corrections.

I

The Challenge of Barth

For some time I have been wrestling with the monumental work of Karl Barth as I have sought to develop an authentically evangelical theology for our day. Having studied with Barth in one of his seminars for foreign students in Basel and having carried on an extensive dialogue with Arthur C. Cochrane, perhaps the foremost authority on Barth in this country and a former colleague of mine at Dubuque Theological Seminary, I have been especially eager to formulate my thoughts on his theology. I confess my indebtedness to him even while finding it necessary to take issue with some of his conclusions, especially in the area of the doctrine of salvation.

Barth's theology is both challenging and disconcerting, particularly to one who stands in the tradition of Protestant evangelicalism. His theological method, which draws upon Anselm ("faith seeking understanding"), presents a solid alternative to both the rationalism and mysticism that dominate much current theology. His doctrines of God and the person of Christ have been a noteworthy and positive influence on my theological development. In my estimation Barth's exposition of the being and perfections of God surpasses that of the Reformers in comprehensiveness, clarity, and biblical fidelity, though this is not to deny that at certain points he can be corrected by them even in this area. I have also greatly benefited from his doctrine of Scripture, though I believe his theory of inspiration to be inadequate. My greatest difficulty has been with his views on salvation, the church, and the sacraments. What he says is illuminating and stimulating, but it has also made me profoundly uneasy.

In my study of Barth I have often wondered why he appears so close at times to the theology of the Protestant Reformation and so far at other times from that tradition. In his earlier years he was known as a neo-Calvinist, but he has acknowledged to me personally that both Calvin and Luther became less important to him as he developed his theology.[1] References to the Reformers abound in all the volumes of his *Church Dogmatics*, but they are much more prevalent in the earlier ones. In spite of his obvious continuity with the Reformation he often manifests a palpably different spirit, which is much more in tune with the modern world. It can be shown that in some areas of doctrine—for example, the ministry, the sacraments, and perhaps also eschatology—Barth has a closer affinity to the left-wing Reformation, particularly the Anabaptists, than to the main-line Reformation. I believe it can also be demonstrated that Barth reflects many of the concerns of the Enlightenment, seen in its broad sense, despite his often severe criticisms of Enlightenment philosophy and the neo-Protestant theology that flowed from it.[2] Moreover, Barth was heavily indebted to Protestant Pietism, not only of the eighteenth century but also of the nineteenth, especially as this is seen in Kierkegaard and Johann Christoph Blumhardt.[3] Schleiermacher, in whom Pietism and the later Enlightenment come together, made a particularly profound impact upon Barth, and though he took sharp issue with Schleiermacher's theology and excluded him from his theological family tree,[4] he could not shake off that influence entirely.

In Barth's divergence from the theology of the Reformers, which is most noticeable in the area of soteriology, he nevertheless appeals to the same criterion—the Word and the Spirit. His doctrine of Scripture is not identical with that of the Reformers and indeed reflects the immeasurable impact of historical criticism, but he has nonetheless endeavored to formulate a theology of the Word of God. At the same time he also tries to develop a theology of universal reconciliation in which the pre-existent and incarnate Christ seems to figure more prominently than the indwelling Christ and in which the triumph of grace effected in the past tends to overshadow the crisis of faith.

Perhaps it can be said that my reservations are aimed not so much at Barth himself as at an exaggerated Barthianism that pictures this world as already effectively redeemed, that sees saving grace present in all world religions, and that regards the sacraments as outmoded and without any value.[5] There are also some who claim that since the world is now reconciled and under the Lordship of Christ, all its undertakings on behalf of humanity are therefore legitimate and merit everyone's support. Barth, of course, must not be identified with these profound misconceptions, but their seeds are definitely to be found in his theology.

Despite his considerable caution and sophistication Barth does not always succeed in holding in balance certain emphases, which therefore gives his theology an objective cast. When he speaks of salvation by faith, for example, it is clear that at least on occasion he means salvation by the faithfulness of God, though this is more the exception than the rule.[6] When he refers to the overcoming of the antithesis between good and evil in Jesus Christ, he generally gives the impression that the antithesis has been done away with and that evil is no more than a phantom in the minds of men; yet in view of his later remarks on a continuing battle between light and darkness, it would seem that this is too sweeping a generalization. In his earlier writings Barth sometimes acknowledges that reconciliation needs to be "completed" in the response of faith,[7] but as he develops his position he sees faith more as a manifestation or evidence of a salvation already completed on the cross of Calvary. Inconsistencies are the bane of every great theologian, and whether they can always be ultimately harmonized is open to question. What is important to understand is that there are at least two strands in Barth on the finality of salvation, and though one is more dominant than the other, both must be taken into consideration if we are to do justice to the breadth and complexity of his thought.

We think it can be shown that in his attempt to cope with the new life- and world-view that stems from the Enlightenment and has continued in considerably modified form into the twentieth century Barth was compelled to use new concepts and fresh imagery in order to restate the historic faith of the church reaffirmed in the Protestant Reformation. Torrance astutely observes that in his dialectical theology "Barth was engaging in a terrific struggle with theological and philosophical language,"[8] and we think this is very true. Barth saw in Kierkegaardian existentialism, with its negations and paradoxes, the vehicle by which he could call the church of his time back to the biblical gospel. He perceived that he had to utter a shattering no to the hubris of modern man and the modern church before he could utter a resounding yes to the goodness of creation and the universality of reconciliation and redemption. He had to expose the attenuated theology of a modernistic Protestantism before he could reconstruct a genuinely evangelical, ecumenical theology that would be solidly anchored in the Scriptures and that would include the valid insights of the great theologians in the Roman Catholic as well as the

Reformation traditions. The theology of crisis or the dialectical theology, with its negations of man in his prideful autonomy,[9] had to precede the theology of the Word of God, with its affirmations of the man in Christ. Whereas the accent in the early Barth had been on the infinite gulf between God and man (à la Kierkegaard), in his maturity he emphasized the analogical relation between God and his creation, though he was insistent that this could be perceived only by faith (*analogia fidei*).

In his theological development Barth was constantly modifying and enlarging his outlook, and this is a tribute to his capacity to engage in self-criticism and to learn anew from the Scriptures and the church tradition. His ideal was not a theology of those who have arrived but a theology of those on the way (*theologia viatorum*). Barth also sought to be open to the light of God in creation and culture, and this accounts for his willingness to learn from the world outside the church.

The distinctly new spirit that we detect in Barth is by no means a compromising spirit and even less a pagan spirit; it is a genuinely Christian spirit that was compelled to be more inclusive than the Reformation dared to be but therefore also more receptive to attitudes and currents of thought that conflict with biblical Christianity. Barth was uncompromising in his fidelity to the message of the gospel as disclosed in Holy Scripture, but in his attempt to make this message intelligible to a post-Christian age, he had to employ insights and symbols drawn from the present as well as the past. Yet in contradistinction to Schleiermacher and Tillich, he was able to elude the pitfalls of a philosophical theology where cultural values obscure and even subvert the message of faith. Barth to his everlasting credit resisted the concerted attempt of cultural Christians to transmute theology into anthropology and to substitute creative spirituality for the evangelical proclamation. At the same time, as a truly modern man he could not avoid the infiltration of various themes and concerns of the culture into his theology; and this means that certain truths of the biblical revelation became necessarily overshadowed by other truths, which for the most part are also fully biblical but more in accord with the spirit of the times or the wisdom of the recent past. In his emphasis on the all-encompassing triumph of grace he remained essentially within the biblical framework, but his vision of an eschatological future without hell and his denial of the devil as a personal being signify a cultural intrusion into a genuinely biblical perspective. His stress on the cosmic Christ now and again tended to overshadow the Jesus Christ of biblical history, though he also sought to maintain the particularity of the biblical revelation.

Barth never wished to become a Barthian, and he wisely saw that his theology too needed to be measured and corrected in the light of Holy Scripture. In the spirit of Barth I have modestly tried to raise questions on whether some of his central affirmations can be substantiated in the light of the revelation to which he himself appealed. As a Reformed theologian I have tried to keep myself open to correction by Barth, and I have been compelled to rethink some of my past positions after wrestling with his deeply original and brilliant insights.

Barth was not a reactionary, and this too redounds to his credit. He perceived that we cannot simply return to past ages and repeat outmoded formulas. We cannot turn our backs upon the modern intellectual and cultural awakening that has given the world some of its greatest literature, art, and music. A flight from culture is not the solution to the problems of the church in our time. Neither is a last-ditch attempt to salvage the credibility of the faith in the face of the attacks of its cultured despisers, since this only betrays a church on the defensive, a church that trusts no longer in the Word of God but in its own methods and powers of persuasion. What is needed is a church that goes forth into the world with the Word of the gospel confident that Christ himself will be victorious in his Word as he has been in the past and that no earthly or demonic power can withstand him. The man of God should seek neither detachment nor separation from the world and its philosophies but rather their transformation and conversion into the service of faith. This was Barth's grand vision, and it is one to which we heartily subscribe.

Barth was always concerned to maintain the

eschatological boundary (*diastasis*) between Christ and culture, but he also saw, as did Calvin, that the world is the theater of God's glory, the field in which the truth of the gospel can be promulgated and demonstrated. In contradistinction to an other-worldly spirituality he believed that the values and creative insights of secular culture could be made to serve either directly or indirectly the righteousness of the kingdom, though not without undergoing some alteration. His surprising openness to the modern world, the robust freedom by which he was able to move and work in an environment that was basically hostile to the Christian message, show that he must be taken seriously by all who wish to be at the same time ambassadors of Jesus Christ and responsible citizens. Whether Barth was sometimes too open to the modern vision and not sufficiently cognizant of the lostness of the world in its present state will occupy much of our attention.

II

Barth's Continuing Relevance

The 1960s witnessed an eclipse of Barthian theology and the rise of theological movements of a faddistic nature. We recall to mind the death-of-God theology, secular theology, the theology of hope, and the theology of revolution. In the past few years we have seen the emergence of third-world theology, black theology, the theology of liberation, and political theology. What is not so well known is that Barth's influence can be discerned in all these movements including the new missiology, which interprets the mission of the church as liberation from economic and political forms of oppression.[1] This is not to say, however, that Barth would endorse the thrust of these new movements. In fact, at certain pivotal points he would find himself in sharp disagreement. We do maintain that many of Barth's creative insights have lived on in these movements, even where the gospel seems to be politicalized or secularized. At the same time a reexamination of Barth's writings could supply a needed corrective to the secularization rampant in the new theology.

Barth was painfully aware of the idolatrous

pretension in revolutionary thought as well as the callous insensitivity to the plight of the poor in the conservatism of the bourgeoisie, and he sought to bring both under the searing judgment of God. It is as much an error to interpret him as an ideologically committed social revolutionary as a product of Swiss middle-class piety.[2] He warned that "we must guard ourselves from the temptation of accepting either a philosophy of revolution or a philosophy of reaction."[3] At the same time, he identified himself as a democratic socialist in his political involvement, and there is no doubt that his sympathies lay with the downtrodden and dispossessed.[4] While a pastor in Safenwill, Switzerland (1911–1921), he laid the groundwork for the organization of labor unions in his community. Yet in his battle against injustice and suffering he denounced not only the exploitation of the workingman by factory owners and managers but also the drinking and gambling addictions of the poor. He had a special concern for those in prison and in the last years of his life conducted preaching services for the prisoners in Basel.

Barth's active resistance to Nazism and the crucial role that he played in the Confessing Church movement in Germany further attest the integral relation between his theology and social and political concerns.[5] Already in June, 1933, a few months after Hitler came to power, Barth issued a pamphlet entitled *Theological Existence Today*, which was an impassioned attack on Hitler's sponsorship of the

German Christians and on the official church for not taking a stand against this encroachment. In December of 1934 Barth was expelled from his professorship at the University of Bonn for refusing to begin his lectures with the Nazi salute "Heil Hitler!"; instead he opened his classes in prayer. Barth was instrumental in organizing Christian resistance to Hitler and was the primary author of the Barmen Confession, which drew sharp lines between the authority of the revelation of Jesus Christ as attested in the Scriptures and other revelations in nature and culture, to which the German Christians appealed. Although he was active in the resistance movement, theology was never replaced by politics as his primary interest. The Barmen Confession was concerned with the purity and integrity of the message of the church and not with the structures of the state as such.

The continuing relevance of Barth can also be seen in the Confession of 1967 in the United Presbyterian Church U.S.A., whose theme is God's work of reconciliation in Jesus Christ and the ministry of reconciliation, and the newly proposed confession in the Presbyterian Church U.S. It is also discernible in *A Plan of Union*, a tentative confessional statement that is geared to bringing together the two Presbyterian churches. In this confession we find these words which definitely bear the imprint of Barthian theology: "The Church of Jesus Christ is the provisional demonstration of what God intends for all humanity."

Despite his strenuous objections to the synergism and sacerdotalism which he believes are endemic to Roman Catholicism, Barth has become increasingly appreciated by Roman Catholic scholars for the breadth of his ecumenical vision, for his openness to dialogue with Christians of other traditions, and for his willingness to subject his own Reformation tradition to the scrutiny of the transcendent criterion of the Word of God, Jesus Christ himself speaking to the whole church through the Scriptures. Among Catholic scholars who have treated Barth sympathetically though not uncritically are B. A. Willems, Jerome Hamer, Henri Bouillard, Hans Urs von Balthasar, and Hans Küng.[6]

Since the publication of Berkouwer's *Triumph of Grace in the Theology of Karl Barth*,[7] there has been considerably more openness to Barth's theology in evangelical circles. G. W. Bromiley, one of the key translators of Barth's *Kirchliche Dogmatik* and professor of historical theology at Fuller Theological Seminary, maintains that Barth can be of immense aid to evangelicals in opening up new vistas in the area of theological method and the doctrines of revelation and Scripture. Other evangelical theologians who have been appreciative of Barth without noticeably compromising the fundamentals of the faith, as these are understood in historic evangelicalism, are Thomas Torrance, David Mueller, Paul Jewett, Bernard Ramm, Klaas Runia, Carl Henry, Colin Brown, and Kenneth Hamilton. I would count myself in this category in that I have tried to be open but still discriminating. Some of the theologians associated with the "evangelical left," which seeks a radical social witness on the basis of biblical faith, have also been strongly influenced by Barth. Here could be mentioned John Howard Yoder, Joseph Bettis, Helmut Gollwitzer, F. Burton Nelson, and Donald Dayton.[8] More negative critics of the Barthian theology who can be broadly classified as "evangelical" are Gustaf Wingren, Fred Klooster, Helmut Thielicke, Emil Brunner, Gordon Clark, Cornelius Van Til, and John Warwick Montgomery. Lately, with the rise of a theology of interpersonal relations in evangelical circles, there have been signs of a reaction in favor of more objectivity in theology, and Barth's position is now being entertained as a viable option. Some even see the Barthian theology as a long-awaited godsend for overcoming the traditional cleavage between modernism and fundamentalism.

Barth's theological impact is especially noticeable in his doctrine of salvation, where he seems to propose something radically new. It is in this area where Evangelicals and also some Roman Catholics take issue with him. His soteriology contains much that stands in continuity with the tradition of the church, but at certain decisive points he breaks with historical orthodoxy.

His insistence that everything that is of any consequence in the religious dimension of man's life has already been accomplished in Christ and that man's response to this salvation is basically ethical not only in the individual but in the social sense has created the climate for the new secular and political theologies. His view that the gospel always sides with the poor over the rich and that its claims must be addressed to the whole of man's life has given added impetus to those movements in the church that seek to promote radical social change. Pacifists have been heartened by his then courageous call for an end to the cold war between West and East and his unequivocal repudiation of weapons of mass extermination.

At the same time Barth's staunch affirmation of the deity of Christ and the efficacy of his atoning sacrifice places him in diametrical opposition to the latest theological trends, which tend to see Jesus as exemplar of the new humanity more than as Savior from sin. His appeal to Scripture over culture in determining spiritual and ethical norms also reveals the chasm between Barth and avant-garde theology. While fully acknowledging the political responsibility of the church, he was adamant that the role of the church is qualitatively different from the role of the state or civil community. Moreover, it should be kept in mind that one of the foremost critics of the new theology, Jacques Ellul, is a faithful though discriminating exponent of Barthian thought.

For Barth the heart of the atonement is not the punishment of sin (though this is not excluded) but the triumph of grace over sin. The principal focus is on the reconciliation of man to God as this has been effected in the life and death of Jesus Christ.

Included in this is the overcoming of sin, death, hell, and the powers of darkness, which have challenged the good creation of God.

On the current scene the emphasis is on the reconciling of nations, races, and classes that find themselves in open and perilous conflict with one another. Barth's emphasis on the reconciliation of man with God in Jesus Christ might serve as the spiritual or theological foundation for the quest for reconciliation on the horizontal level. Whether the new theology is open to radical revision in the light of the Barthian corrective is a question that will not concern us in this volume. On the other hand whether Barth's doctrine of reconciliation and re- demption is itself a faithful expression of the scriptural teaching on this subject and of the consensus of the church tradition, especially of the Reformation tradition, is quite another matter, and we shall try to answer this as best we can.

It is very possible that with the decline of social activism and an anticipated growing disenchant- ment with mysticism and occultism, the 1980s may experience a revival of the neo-orthodoxy associated with the names of Karl Barth and Emil Brunner. In a desperate attempt to escape from the morass of subjectivism and relativism, young people espe- cially, both in the church and out, may very well strive to regain objectivity in religion and continuity with the theological traditions of the past. Signs of a movement in this direction can even now be detected. It is indisputable that in a reaction against utopianism many young people are already seeking a more realistic attitude toward life and the world. This is not to discount the utopian or chiliastic elements in Barth's theology,[9] but they are counter-balanced by a biblical realism that refuses to identify cultural breakthroughs toward a higher degree of justice with the eschatological kingdom of God. Our hope is that a new theology will emerge that will be genuinely evangelical and catholic in scope, that will affirm both the Word and the Spirit as revealed to us in the depths of our inner being.

Karl Barth's theology just as it stands cannot be the answer for the church of tomorrow, since it is too one-sided in its emphasis on the rational over the mystical and sacramental. Moreover, its focus is primarily on the Germanic scene and shows little acquaintance with the evangelicalism of the English-speaking world, which at its best sought to hold in balance the objective-historical and subjective-mystical dimensions of salvation (as in the theology of Jonathan Edwards).[10] It also manifests little evidence of an in-depth encounter with the Eastern Orthodox church, especially in its modern form. Yet the theology of tomorrow can ill afford to neglect Barth's outstanding contribution, and the battles that he fought and won will have to be recognized and appreciated by any new theology that seeks to be at the same time evangelical and catholic. The theology of tomorrow cannot simply return to a pre-Barthian stance, for this is neither desirable nor possible. A truly ecumenical and evangelical theology will be a fruit of the Barthian revolution, but at the same time it will seek to transcend the limitations and ambiguities of the Barthian theology if it is to be a viable option for the church of the future.

III

The Objectivistic Slant

Where Barth's soteriology stands in most obvious tension with that of historical evangelical orthodoxy is in its objectivism. He affirms that all men are elected by God and adopted into sonship in his eternal decree that comes to historical realization in Jesus Christ. All are predestined to salvation in Christ even before the dawning of history, even before the primordial fall of man.[1] Moreover, all persons are created in Christ, and creation itself is an irrefragable sign of predestination, a decisive step in the plan of salvation. God's predestination is revealed and fulfilled in the coming of Jesus Christ into worldly history. This One whose origin is in heaven is both the rejected and the elected in that he bears the burden of God's wrath against sin and at the same time realizes and epitomizes the promise of salvation for all mankind. He includes within himself the divine condemnation of sin and the predestined liberation of the sinner. In him we are justified, reconciled, and redeemed.

Barth sees the drama of salvation in three stages: creation, reconciliation, and redemption.[2] Already at creation the Nothingness or the chaos was decisively defeated and rendered impotent, and God's plan for the salvation and glorification of his children was put into effect. Creation "commences and culminates in light," and this is why his revelation is never absolutely new, since it restores and renews what was already begun in creation.[3] The saving action of God was fulfilled in the incarnation and atonement of Jesus Christ, for in him we see man reconciled and restored to God. The work of the Holy Spirit is to awaken people to this decisive fact and to bring them into accord with God's purpose declared in Jesus Christ. Barth calls this the work of redemption, though redemption in its objective aspect is included in reconciliation, and in its eschatological aspect is still a future reality, since the universal revelation of what God has done in Christ has yet to occur.

For Barth the final and decisive event of salvation is in the past, in the history of Jesus Christ, though it awaits its full manifestation. This objectivistic bent can be seen in the following statements:

As the one thing which has to be done it is already wholly and utterly accomplished in Him [Jesus Christ]. As that which has taken place in God—in which we are indeed participators on the strength of the nature of the person and work of Jesus Christ—it is in itself and from the very outset something which has taken place to and in us.[4]

Again, the act of God accomplished and expressed in Jesus Christ is the justification and sanctification of man. It is thus the act in which man, whether he realises it or not, is objectively alienated, separated and torn away from this resisting element in him, because he is already set in the liberty of the children of God.[5]

The event of redemption took place then and there in Him, and therefore "for us.". . . It calls us to discipleship, but not in such a way that it becomes an event of redemption only through our obedience to this call. . . . It [redemption] has happened fully and exclusively in Him, excluding any need for completion.[6]

Their [the Christians'] saving death took place, not now and here, but in supreme actuality then and there, when they, too, were baptized in and with Jesus' baptism of death. . . .[7]

What Barth is affirming is that reconciliation, the restoration of man to communion with God, was effectively and totally accomplished in the sacrificial life and death of Jesus Christ. The reconciling work of God entails the "healing of the rent," the "closing of the mortal wound, from which humanity . . . suffers."[8] It includes the justification and sanctification of a fallen human race that has become alienated from God. It also involves the calling of all men into the service of the kingdom of God and their adoption into his sonship. The "whole reconciliation, the whole restoration of peace, between man and God"[9] was effected when God became man in Jesus Christ and identified himself with our sin and travail.[10] The "transformation" that will occur at the end of history "has already taken place in His life and death and resurrection."[11] Yet to see and know Jesus Christ and the glory of his redemption there has to be a penetration and removal of the veil that hides the significance of the Christ event. This removal has not yet taken place for the human race as a whole, but in faith we can gain an awareness of our salvation in Christ though not a direct and comprehensive knowledge of it.

This brings us to the subjective dimension of salvation—faith, which is both a work of the Spirit within us and a work of the human subject who is acted upon by grace. Faith for Barth is an acknowledgment of God's act of love in Christ and obedience to its imperatives. Faith includes both cognitive and ethical dimensions, but it must not be confused with the redemptive event itself. Faith in itself is not the redemptive act of God but the awakening to the significance of this act. It is also obedience in the light of this act. Faith is a gift of grace in that man on his own cannot believe or assent to the truth of the biblical revelation. Yet through grace man is made active and is empowered to trust and obey. We are justified by faith alone (*sola fide*) in the sense that only in faith can we perceive and apprehend our justification and the justification of all people accomplished in Jesus Christ.

It might be thought that his doctrine of conversion would be essentially concerned with the subjective response to salvation, but Barth also sees conversion in objectivistic terms though without denying its subjective dimension.

We ask where and when there has taken place, takes place and will take place, as an actual event, this movement of man in the totality and with the radical dispute in which the old man dies and the new arises, this liberation by God's free grace. And the answer is simply that in the strict sense it is an actual event only in Him, in His life, in His obedience as the true Son of God and true Son of Man.[12]

The divine change, the conversion of man to God, was effected in the history of Jesus Christ. "This change which God has made [in Christ] is in truth man's liberation. It comes upon him wholly from without, from God. Nevertheless, it is his liberation."[13] He can even say: "In His [Christ's] death there took place the regeneration and conversion of man."[14] Barth empathizes with the nineteenth-century German Reformed pastor Kohlbrügge, who said that "he was converted on Golgotha."[15] In the kind of theology propounded by Barth one becomes a Christian at Calvary: there in the passion and death of our Lord Christian life begins. It is at Calvary that we and all humankind have passed from death to life.

At the same time Barth acknowledges that conversion must also take place in the subjective sphere as a correspondence to what happened to man in the objective sphere.[16] Yet this conversion is incomplete and rudimentary, whereas the conversion that took place in Christ is perfect and holds good for all times. Barth says that we see in the Bible not "converted men" but "men caught up in the movement of conversion."[17] The conversion enacted by the Holy Spirit in the lives of men is "neither exhausted in a once-for-all act, nor is it accomplished in a series of such acts." [18] "At each moment of its occurrence it is itself another change, a conversion, which calls for even more radical conversion." [19]

Conversion means not the laying hold of a new freedom that was simply not present hitherto but the exercise of a freedom "which he does not need to assume or give to himself because this is not necessary, since it has been already given in what God has long since done for the world." [20] Barth declares: "The Word of grace simply tells him that the table is spread for him and for all, but that a few places—his own included—are still vacant, and would he be so good as to sit down and fall to, instead of standing about and cleverly or foolishly prattling." [21]

Given the logic of his position it would appear that all persons are in Christ, and Barth often gives this unmistakable impression. Yet he makes clear that though all are elected to be "in Christ," not all are "in Christ" *de facto* in the sense that "what happened for them had also happened to them and in them." [22] In another sense, however, Barth does speak of all being "in Christ," since Jesus Christ embodies and represents the whole human race, and consequently what has taken place in him also happens to all others. Moreover, his grace reaches out to all, and his dominion includes all, though not all have been inwardly enlightened concerning their favored status in the eyes of God. Barth declares:

"He, the living Jesus Christ, is the circle enclosing all men and every man and closed in Christian faith— the circle of divine judgment and divine grace."[23] This statement implies that all are virtually in Christ, that all are in Christ *de jure*, and this seems to be Barth's intent. Perhaps it can be said that for Barth all are in Christ by virtue of their creation through Christ and the universal atonement of Christ, but Christ is not yet in all men in that his Spirit has been poured out only on some.

In speaking of the elect, Barth can surprisingly say that "we cannot equate their number with the totality of all men"; to do so is to confuse God's sovereign grace with a universalistic principle.[24] It is also to overlook the incontestable fact that some reject the salvation of Jesus Christ. Yet for Barth all persons are under the sign of election, all are claimed by the new reality that has invaded the world of sin and darkness, and no one can escape from or ignore this claim. We can regard every person optimistically, since all have an Advocate and Intercessor in Jesus Christ, against whose omnipotent love the gates of hell cannot prevail (Matt. 16:18). For Barth no limitation can be imposed on God's illimitable grace, which breaks through every human defense.

Barth's understanding of the *ordo salutis* (order of salvation) also reflects an objectivistic stance. In traditional Protestant orthodoxy the *ordo salutis* connotes sharply distinguishable steps in the salvific process: a demarcation is often made between justification, calling, regeneration, conversion, sanctification, etc. Barth sees the *ordo salutis* as different moments of the one redemptive occurrence of the humiliation and incarnation of Jesus Christ, an occurrence that has its foundation in eternity and its realization in time.[25] Election, conversion, reconciliation, and redemption are all aspects of the eternal decision of Jesus Christ to identify and unite himself with fallen humanity. Justification and sanctification are not two separate divine actions but facets of the event of reconciliation, though he does not identify them. Faith is simply the subjective response to the one event of salvation, which encompasses election, reconciliation, calling, conversion, etc.

At the same time a case could be made that Barth does have an order of salvation after a fashion in that he sees the eternal decision of Jesus Christ unfolded in creation and reconciliation and culminating in an eschatological redemption. His stress is on the simultaneity of the one act of salvation, but he nevertheless seems to affirm a temporal sequence in his distinction between creation, reconciliation, and the eschatological fulfillment (*Vollendung*).

Barth's objectivistic soteriology can be rightly understood only against the background of his theory of evil. While recognizing the objective reality of evil, he is adamant that it has no solid basis in eternity. Evil has no positive ontological status and exists only because of God's act of negation. It is given a provisional reality by virtue of the fact that it is that which God does not will. He calls evil the

39

chaos or the Nothingness (*das Nichtige*).[26] It is "the impossible which is excluded by reality."[27] Already at the beginning of things God excluded the Nothingness from the domain of his creation, though it infiltrates the creation through the spell that it casts upon men's minds. Yet in Jesus Christ the whole sphere of evil "has already been overcome"; it is something "which has been destroyed by the positive will of God's overflowing glory."[28] "Because Jesus is Victor, nothingness is routed and extirpated."[29] With Augustine and against Leibniz Barth sees evil not simply as *privatio* but as an assault upon goodness. Nothingness, he says, has its own dynamic, the "dynamic of damage and destruction."[30] The chaos is a ruinous and destructive power, but its power lies in negation and subtraction. It continues to have a semblance of power even after the work of Christ, but this is only because of its capability to deceive. In itself it has been done away with, though men cannot perceive its basis in illusion until they have been freed by the light of the Christ revelation.

The devil, for Barth, is not a personal being but nonbeing. It is termed "hypostatised falsehood" and "the resisting element in man."[31] The devil is the chaos in its dynamic manifestation. Barth does not see, as Luther did, that the devil also partakes in the Holy. Luther even addressed the devil on occasion as "thou holy devil." In the tradition of historical orthodoxy the devil is a fallen angel and thereby has superhuman intelligence and real power. I contend

against Barth that the demonic includes both destructive and creative elements. The devil does not
have the status of deity, but he contains godlike
elements. As a "divine anti-divine being" (Tillich)
he can be an adversary to God as well as to man.[32]
Barth denies that the devil is a genuine adversary of
God, though he is treated as such by Jesus Christ,
who identifies himself with mankind in its struggle
against evil.[33] In Christ God makes the cause of the
creature his own and defeats and overcomes the
demonic hosts on the plane of humanity. In the
events of the cross and resurrection God reveals and
confirms his undisputed hegemony over all creaturely powers as well as the uncreated darkness,
which exists only by his negation.[34] Man in and of
himself is no match for the Nothingness, but the
latter is no threat to God, who has rendered it
powerless in the light of the cross of Christ. Indeed,
even at the creation God's no had reduced Nothingness to impotence. "God does not have to contend
with it [the chaos] for the mastery. . . . For as soon as
it entered the world it came under His dominion."[35]

In summary, for Barth, evil is real, but it does not
exist in any substantial sense. It exists, but not as
God and the world exist. He sometimes describes it
as "nonexistent," "insubstantial," and "empty." It
has a parasitical existence, since its reality is
dependent on its capability of corrupting the good. It
persists as an illusion that deceives and poisons the
world of humanity. Barth sees no strategy of evil
planned by a supernatural personal evil power, but

instead the anarchy of chaos and disorder that threatens the order and well-being of God's creation. Yet these threats have been totally and permanently dispelled by the momentous victory of Jesus Christ. Man's slowness in recognizing this victory accounts for the still persistent shadow it casts over the history of man. It can still work havoc not because it has creative ontological power but because man in his sin prefers fearing evil to trusting God. But man need not fear, since the Nothingness has been unmasked as the illusion that it is by the death and resurrection of Jesus Christ. Its sham and powerlessness have been forever exposed by the humiliation and exaltation of the Son of God. The demons have been routed, though this fact is known only to faith. Light now shines in the world of darkness, but this light is not always perceived because of man's still blinded eyes.

IV

Reinterpreting the Atonement

All the mainline views on the atonement are to be found in Barth in some degree or other, but he brings into the picture something new. He does not abandon traditional concepts such as substitution, satisfaction, and penal redemption (despite what Arnold Come alleges), but he sees them in a new context. He deepens and radicalizes their meaning.

There is no doubt that Barth's basic affinity is with the so-called classic or dramatic view of the atonement, in which Jesus Christ is depicted as victor over the powers of darkness.[1] Barth hails Christ as the "Redeemer from sin and death and the devil."[2] The "atonement is God's triumph in the antithesis, in the opposition of man to Himself."[3] It is not a human sacrifice as such but the Word of God Incarnate who overcomes this antithesis, who dispels the tyrants that hold man in subjection. The redemptive work is accomplished by the Son of God through the Manhood of Jesus as his instrument. Barth rejects the view of God being reconciled by Christ as an intermediary between God and man. In his perspective God is the Reconciler, and man is the reconciled.[4]

While there can be no disputing the essential continuity between Barth's position on the atonement and the classical view, he goes beyond it at various points. One area of divergence is that the idea of ransom is definitely underplayed. In his theology the devil has no rights over man, and therefore a transaction with the devil (as in some of the patristic fathers) is unthinkable. He refutes the idea that the devil is "a real antagonist to the living God."[5] The cross of Christ does not so much overthrow the devil as it reveals his decisive defeat and collapse, which already had taken place at the creation and was further implemented at the incarnation. It should also be kept in mind that in Barth the conflict is not with the devil as a personal being but with the Nothingness or chaos of which the devil is a symbolic representation.

Barth's emphasis on the incarnation and resurrection of Christ further allies him with the classic view. In the Latin theory, as enunciated by Anselm, there is a discontinuity between the incarnation and the atonement, since the atoning sacrifice is made by Jesus as man. Barth concurs with the early fathers that the great work of reconciliation was already put into effect at the incarnation of Christ, and it was revealed and fulfilled in the cross and resurrection of Christ. The resurrection and ascension of Christ are the revelation of the work that was completed in his life and death.

Though Barth sees the heart of the atonement in the triumph of Christ over the powers of sin and death and the restoration of communion between God and man, he also makes a place for ideas that are peculiarly associated with the satisfactionist theory of the atonement. Barth is critical of Anselm's view, which pictures God's wounded honor as being propitiated by the sacrifice of a sinless man, but he is nevertheless unwilling to discard the element of truth in the concepts of satisfaction and propitiation. God is not only love but also light, absolute moral holiness; and this means that sin must be judged, punished, and expiated. Barth declares: "And in this place He [Jesus Christ] has not only borne man's enmity against God's grace, revealing it in all its depth. He has borne the far greater burden, the righteous wrath of God against those who are enemies of His grace, the wrath which must fall on us."[6] And again: "In His own Word made flesh, God hears that satisfaction has been done to His righteousness, that the consequences of human sin have been borne and expiated, and therefore that they have been taken away from man—the man for whose sake Jesus Christ intervened."[7] He speaks of the "expiation" of the "enmity in which man as such stands against grace."[8] He also says that Christ was "laden with our sin" and "suffered the punishment for our sin."[9]

Yet in Barth's thought can be seen a profound divergence from the satisfactionist or juridical view, which was accepted with only slight modification in

Protestant orthodoxy. For Barth God's forgiveness is not conditional upon a prior satisfaction for the hurt done to his glory, but this forgiveness itself satisfied the demands of his righteousness.[10] The cross is to be understood primarily not as the fulfillment of a legal contract calling for the shedding of innocent blood but as the triumph of sovereign love over enmity and alienation, which invariably resulted in the shedding of blood. The sacrifice is performed not simply by Jesus as man but by the Son of God in the form of man. It is consequently a divine self-sacrifice: God not only demands but also makes the offering. In this perfect sacrifice the Old Testament sacrificial system is both fulfilled and superseded.

Barth opposes the popular view that through the propitiatory offering of Jesus God changed from wrath to love. Instead he insists (in apparent agreement with Luther) that the work of Christ presupposes and does not create a gracious God. God's wrath is not appeased or turned away by the blood sacrifice of Jesus: it is precisely in this sacrifice that his wrath is revealed—but as the obverse side of his love. The wrath of God is the purity and holiness of his love that will forgive at the cost of utter self-sacrifice but at the same time will never condone any compromise with sin. God's wrath is therefore a means of grace as well as of judgment.[11]

Barth does not generally speak in terms of penal redemption. For him the heart of the atonement is reconciliation, and redemption is more an eschatological concept. At the same time the idea that

Christ takes upon himself the curse or penalty of our sin is very pronounced. Christ is sometimes depicted as the reprobate or the rejected upon whom falls the severity of God's judgment against sin. He can say that "on Him there now comes what ought to come on us: the condemnation of sin in the flesh." [12] And again: "He elects Jesus ... at the head and in the place of all others. The wrath of God, the judgment and the penalty, fall, then, upon Him." [13] This indicates not a discarding but a radicalizing of the concept of penal redemption.

In Barth's theory satisfaction, justification, and sanctification are aspects of the same event, and here again he echoes the position of the church fathers and also of Luther. In the Latin theory, as seen in a dominant strand in Roman Catholic and Protestant orthodoxy, satisfaction, justification, and sanctification are separate or discontinuous acts. Our justification and sanctification are contingent upon the satisfaction done to the honor and justice of God.

In the Anselmian view God receives compensation for Christ's death. The superfluous merit earned by the man Christ is credited to his brethren. In the Barthian view Christ's death is a revelation that God's forgiveness is assured to all men despite their demerits; it is an incomparable and efficacious sign that all men are now included in the kingdom of his righteousness. The message of the cross is not that merits are now available to the sinner that satisfy the law of distributive justice; rather the cross proclaims that God's grace goes beyond the strict requirements of justice, that the law of retribution has been both duly met and abrogated by the forgiving love of God.[14] The cross is basically to be understood not as a ritually prescribed instrument of propitiation directed to eternity but as an incursion of divine grace into the arena of human history. The cross reveals that God has identified himself with our sin and misery and has thereby overcome and expelled the powers of sin, guilt, and death. Barth says that we are saved not from the hand of God but by his hand,[15] even though this first note is not denied when seen in its proper context.

Barth's synthesis of the classic and Latin views of the atonement can be seen in the following remark: "He [Jesus Christ] could reveal Himself at once as the One who as the servant of all bore the punishment of death which we had deserved, and the One who as the Lord of all took from death its power and for ever vanquished and destroyed it."[16] Jesus is both the Lamb of God who is the sacrifice for our sins and the Lion of Judah (cf. Rev. 5:5) who triumphs over our sins.

While there are admitted tensions between Barth's position and the Latin view, there is open conflict between his position and the subjective or moral influence theory of the atonement. In this view, which was espoused by Schleiermacher and Ritschl, reconciliation is an interior change in man that occurs in the confrontation with the love of God as revealed in Jesus Christ. Jesus is the revealer and exemplar of divine love rather than an atonement for sin. Barth on the contrary holds that reconciliation is not so much a change in the attitude of man as a change in the human situation resulting from a new initiative on the part of God toward man. On the other hand, it is misleading to aver, as does much traditional theology, that there was a substantial change in God's attitude toward man—from antipathy and rage to compassion.[17] Instead we must contend that God's kindness and severity (cf. Rom. 11:22) were both manifested in Jesus Christ, and that through his loving and condemning action alienation and brokenness were overcome. Reconciliation indicates that a new basis has been established for a fruitful and enduring relationship between God and man. Moreover, the reconciliation that Christ brings was prior to the cross, though it was manifested and fulfilled in the cross. It has its source in the incarnation and even before the incarnation in the eternal counsel of God. The life and death of Jesus Christ reveal the justification of God as well as the justification of man. God not only discloses and communicates his righteousness to man in the life and death of Christ, but he also vindicates his righteousness. God justifies himself in the justification which he pronounces upon man.

Barth does not deny the subjective dimension of the atonement, but he sees this basically as the apprehension and acknowledgment of the reconciliation already given in Jesus Christ. Man is already placed in the sphere of salvation through the atoning work of Jesus Christ, and he needs only to acknowledge his changed condition. It is as if man were set on an escalator to heaven. He can walk backward, which is ultimately self-defeating and frustrating, but he cannot alter his condition. He can close his eyes to the light that now shines upon him, but he cannot dispel this light.

Barth's objectivistic and universalistic penchant can be seen in the peculiar twist that he gives to the concept of substitutionary atonement, as presented in his *Church Dogmatics* IV, 1 and 2. In contradistinction to historical orthodoxy he affirms not a unilateral substitution but rather an "exchange" whereby God condescends to man while man is taken up in the unity of the life of Jesus Christ. Whereas the humiliation is peculiarly associated with and manifested in the divine nature of Christ,[18] the exaltation is realized in his human nature.[19] In the self-sacrificing Son of God, who takes upon himself the burden of our sin and guilt, mankind is crucified and buried. In the triumphant Son of Man, who upholds and participates in the lordship and glory of God, mankind is exalted not as God but to God, to fellowship with him. The substitution is not a work that takes place outside of us and is then subsequently applied to us but a work in which our dying and rising again is enacted. It is not that Christ has borne the judgment of God in our place, thereby enabling us to escape judgment. Instead the judgment has been executed upon us in Christ, and therefore we and all men have already passed through this judgment.[20] Salvation is not the imputation of the alien righteousness of Christ to those who believe (as in Luther) but the entering into a righteousness that has now become our own and that rightly belongs to all humanity.[21] What occurs in the cross is more than the defeat of sin and the vindication of righteousness: there sin is removed from the life of man and replaced by righteousness. Berkouwer observes that for Barth the substitution lies not in the traditional "not we, but He" but in the destruction of the old man and the resurrection of the new.[22] The man of sin is wiped out, and the new man, in whom we are all included, is raised in his place.

Jesus Christ is portrayed as both our Substitute and our Representative, but these terms are laden with new meaning.[23] He suffers the punishment of sin on our behalf, but only in a qualified sense can it be said that he suffers and dies in our stead, since we suffer and die in and with him. The substitutionary atonement connotes not so much the purchase of salvation by the blood of Christ (though he does not discount this motif) as the conversion of man to salvation in the death and resurrection of Christ. Barth does not break completely with the traditional understanding of substitution, but he reinterprets it in such a way that it appears that not only the objective but also the subjective change has taken place in Jesus Christ. His position is that in the life and death of Jesus Christ a dramatic reversal has occurred in man's history and destiny irrespective of his attitude or response. Barth sees in the event of the atonement not simply the removal of the penalty of sin but the renewal of the world.

A second area of difference between Barth's conception and that of much traditional theology is that he depicts reconciliation as having been accomplished in the act of humiliation and incarnation.[24] The cross and resurrection simply confirm and reveal what has already taken place. He also speaks of these events as the climactic unfolding of the eternal decision of the Son of God to unite himself with human flesh for the sake of our salvation.

We now come to Barth's view that the events of the atonement happen in the realm of sacred or inner history (Geschichte), not objectively discernible history (Historie); only the latter is available to empirical investigation. It was possible to observe the crucifixion but not the reconciling work of Christ, which is hidden from all sight and understanding. "The atonement which occurred in Him," he says, "is an invisible atonement which is contrasted with any soul-and-sense relationship between us and Jesus as impossibility is contrasted with possibility, death with life, non-existence with existence."[25] The empty tomb was accessible to sight but not the reality of the risen Christ,who was manifest only to those who believed. Some critics of Barth see here a Kantian influence, since for Kant the noumenal realm, the realm of essences, is inaccessible to man's sight and reason. Man can directly perceive only the phenomenal realm, the realm of appearance.[26] It seems that the decisive events of salvation occur in the noumenal, not the phenomenal realm. Yet we believe that Barth is here profoundly biblical in his asseveration that only faith can discern the supernatural reality and mystery that lie within and behind the historical events related to Jesus' life, death, and rising again. He is saying not that these events did not happen in space and time but instead that their divine significance was not obvious or self-evident. The historical critic can show the probability of the crucifixion of Christ and even amass evidential support for the fact that the disciples experienced the creative impact of his personality beyond death. Yet only faith can confess that Christ died for our sins and that his blood cleanses us from all iniquity. Only faith can affirm that Christ rose from the dead for our justification and that he ascended into heaven as our Advocate and Intercessor.

Of theologians in the Anglo-Saxon world P. T. Forsyth probably comes closest to Barth's doctrine of the atonement. Yet even here there are differences, some of which we shall enumerate. Forsyth, like Barth, makes a place for both the triumphal and juridical aspects of the atonement and tends to give precedence to the former.[27] He sees the cross as "the moral conquest of the world's evil, amid the extreme conditions of sin and suffering, by a Victor who had a capital solidarity with the race, and not merely an individual connection with it."[28] He concurs with Barth that the death of Christ is organically related to his whole personal life and action, but his emphasis is decidedly on the cross over the incarnation. As in Barth, reconciliation is regarded as the leitmotif of the atonement. It is said to be mutual in the sense that it involves both sides. Barth does not deny this aspect of the atonement, but for him Jesus Christ represents man's side as well as God's. Forsyth too can speak in this way, but more than Barth he emphasizes that reconciliation must have concrete effects in the lives of God's people here and now. Again like Barth he also sees a regenerative aspect to the atonement, but he would not say that our regeneration has taken place completely outside ourselves in the life and death of Jesus Christ. For Forsyth regeneration takes effect in the church, though it has its source and mainspring in the cross of Christ. Yet he insists that Christ creates in us what he has promised. Barth makes a place for this truth in his doctrine of the Holy Spirit.

With Barth, Forsyth accentuates the objective and accomplished work of Jesus Christ. The reconciling and atoning work of Christ is complete, though it must bear spiritual and ethical fruit in the lives of men. Reconciliation is fundamentally a once-for-all event that alters the human situation and not a process in which man becomes ever more acceptable to God. Forsyth can even say that the whole world, the human race in its entirety, has been redeemed through the cross of Christ: "We are spiritually in a reconciled world, we are not merely in a world in process of empirical reconciliation."[29] In Forsyth's view reconciliation involves a change in God as well—not in his feeling toward man, but in his treatment of man. God's practical relation to us had to be altered in order for him to deal with us as sons rather than transgressors. This is in basic accord with Barth's theology, though he would not express it in just this way.

Again in agreement with Barth, Forsyth seeks to make a place for the concepts of satisfaction, substitution, and penal redemption, though he sees these in a drastically new context. In stark contrast to Schleiermacher and Ritschl he gives prominent attention to the judgment and wrath of God. "The blood of Christ," he says, "stands not simply for the sting of sin on God but the scourge of God on sin, not simply for God's sorrow over sin but for God's wrath on sin."[30] He points to the need for satisfying the righteousness of God, but this satisfaction is made not by Jesus as man but by the Son of God himself. In his words: "It is an offering primarily, not of pity but of sanctity, and neither by God to man nor by man to God, but God to God, the self-sacrifice of the perfectly holy Son to the perfect holiness of the Father."[31] Christ "entered the penumbra of judgment, and from it He confessed in free action . . . before the world, and on the scale of all the world, the holiness of God."[32] Forsyth, unlike Barth, is reluctant to assert that the punishment that sinful man deserves was placed on Christ, though he does concur that Christ freely bore the penalty of sin. Even more than Barth he emphasizes that holiness pertains to the very essence of deity and in contrast to

55

him tends to subordinate the divine love to the divine holiness.

Forsyth refers to the cross as "the great confessional," meaning that there Christ confesses the heinousness of sin and the holiness of God in his judgment on sin. This sacrifice is not penal in the sense that Christ suffers the very condemnation that men in their sin deserve to suffer. Yet Christ's solidarity with man and confession on behalf of man is accepted by God as a proper sacrifice, one in keeping with the moral order of the universe. Here can be seen the influence of J. McLeod Campbell's moral satisfaction theory in which the idea of representative repentance supplants that of penal substitution. For Campbell the vicarious repentance was offered to the Father by the Son, who *"seeing sin and sinners with God's eyes, and feeling with reference to them as God's heart"* made *"a perfect Amen in humanity to the judgment of God on the sin of man."* [33] While acknowledging his debt to Campbell, Forsyth believes that he places undue weight upon Christ's confession of human sin (which in a certain sense the sinless Christ could not do). Also unlike Campbell, Forsyth does not shrink from calling Christ's death "a penal sacrifice," though, as has been indicated, this concept is considerably qualified in his thought.

R. Swanton significantly argues that Campbell's theory is reflected in Barth, though he acknowledges that there is no evidence that Barth was directly affected by either Campbell or Forsyth.[34] This contention has some merit, since Barth too speaks of the solidarity of Christ with fallen mankind and of the perfect penitence of the Son that is offered to the Father. Barth even says in language that might cause difficulty for Campbell and even more for Forsyth: "In the one Israelite Jesus it was God Himself who as the Son of the Father made Himself the object of this accusation and willed to confess Himself a sinner, and to be regarded and dealt with as such."[35] Also in general accord with Campbell, Barth sees the forgiving love of God as prior to the atonement and the atonement as the form of the manifestation of this love, but not its cause. Yet Barth is much more Reformed in his view that Christ suffered not only to satisfy the moral sense of the universe through a demonstration of sympathetic love but also and above all to meet the harsh demands of divine justice. This means that Christ did more than empathize with the sinner: he bore the punishment of our sin.[36] It should be kept in mind, of course, that the theory of representative repentance is only one strand in both Forsyth and Barth.

Barth and Forsyth stand together in affirming the vicarious substitutionary sacrifice of Christ, though both see this sacrifice as something far deeper than mere substitution. I believe that Barth would feel comfortable with this statement of his Scottish peer:

Whatever we mean . . . by substitution, it is something more than merely vicarious. It is certainly not something done over our heads. It is representative. Yet not by the will of man choosing Christ, but by the will of Christ choosing man, and freely identifying Himself with man. It is a matter not so much of substitutionary expiation (which, as these words are commonly understood, leaves us too little committed), but of solidary confession and praise from amid the judgment fires, where the Son of God walks with creative sympathy of the holy among the sinful sons of men.[37]

The two theologians also agree that Christ suffered in his divine as well as his human nature. Since for both men the reconciling and regenerative work was done by the Godhead itself and not by the Son alone, this means that the very God himself was affected by the pain and distress of the creation. While Forsyth refers to the "moral sympathy" of God, Barth speaks of the "sorrow" in the heart of God. The fact that the majestic God himself enters into our suffering and tribulation does not detract from his omnipotence, since he has voluntarily limited himself in order to be with and for his children. This view sharply challenges the traditional doctrine of the impassibility of God.[38]

In summary Barth affirms that God himself is the source and agent of our reconciliation.[39] God took the initiative in our salvation and also carried through. He identified himself with our plight and misery in the person of his Son, Jesus Christ. He triumphed over the powers that enslave us and all people in the cross and resurrection of Christ. His atonement is universal in its scope and efficacy, though this efficacy is manifested now only in the community of faith. This atoning and reconciling work of Christ is completed. Man no longer needs to make reparations for his sins, since this has been taken care of in Christ. He is no longer under the iron law of retribution, since this has been abrogated by the grace of Christ. But man needs to acknowledge his reconciliation and live as one who is reconciled and liberated. He is summoned to bear witness to the Crucified in a life marked by crucifixion.[40] Man, all men, are now under grace, but the Spirit of God has not yet brought this great fact to light in the lives of all. The atoning work of Christ is finished, and this includes all that is necessary for our salvation and future redemption. Even our glorification is a finished work, since it took place in Jesus Christ. But the light that shone in Christ has still to permeate the whole creation. And this is why reconciliation must be fulfilled in a future redemption, even though this eschatological consummation was already antici-pated in the glory that was present in Christ. The glory that is ours is yet to be revealed for all to see.[41]

V

Universal Salvation?

Berkouwer has observed that the principal theme of Barth's theology is the triumph of grace.[1] Barth does not reject this characterization of his thought but prefers Johann Christoph Blumhardt's formula "Jesus is Victor!" (*"Jesus ist Sieger!"*). This means that in Jesus Christ the victory over the powers of darkness was forever secured and that the whole world is now claimed for his kingdom. It also implies that the efficacy of this victory extends throughout human history in the ongoing struggle against sin and its consequences. Despite the unfaithfulness of every man, Christ "creates in the history of every man the beginning of his new history," the opening up of a new horizon to which man himself may still be oblivious.[2]

According to Barth there is only one covenant, that of grace, and only one kind of grace—that of redemption. The providential grace of the Father and the saving grace of the Son are not to be separated and at times are virtually equated, since both have as their goal the redemption of mankind. Preservation is reinterpreted to mean salvation from the power of the chaos.

Also in this theology there is only one kingdom to be reckoned with, only one that has any abiding meaning—the kingdom of Christ. The kingdom of darkness has been radically destroyed and exists only as a shadow kingdom. Barth asserts that "this kingdom is behind us and all men. We and all men are released from . . . this prison."[3] The locus of its present power is in the minds of men, but the kingdom of Christ actually rules over men. The kingdom of Satan is a pseudokingdom with its ambassadors having been disarmed. The world is no longer bewitched but exorcised. It is not a world in slavery but a liberated world, one that wholly and solely belongs to its only Lord and Master, Jesus Christ.

Even those who refuse to acknowledge the reign of Christ find themselves in the domain of his kingdom:

Those who in themselves are disobedient are claimed and absorbed by the act of His obedience. The kingdom which has come to them in all its strangeness is the reality which is so transcendent and efficacious to them that it cannot remain a merely external fact hanging over them. They themselves have to be within it. It is necessarily made their own.[4]

At the same time Barth recognizes that man can and does defy and resist God's grace. "Where the opposition [of men to God] does not break down in faith in the Son given," he says, "even the love of God must itself be destructive."[5] This brings us to the question of whether Barth is in fact a universalist. Joseph Bettis maintains that Barth should not be so categorized, since, though holding to universal election and a universal atonement, he stops short of affirming a universal final salvation and allows for the "impossible possibility" of self-damnation.[6] Emil Brunner on the other hand is convinced that Barth is one of the most thoroughgoing universalists in his insistence that all mankind has already been saved through the cross and resurrection of Jesus Christ. It is true that Barth often speaks in this way, but he can also make this assertion: "Nowhere does the New Testament say that the world is saved, nor can we say that it is without doing violence to the New Testament."[7]

It should be recognized that Barth himself explicitly opposes the doctrine of an inevitable universal restoration of all things to God (apokatastasis). This would tie the grace of God to a law or principle and thereby compromise his sovereign freedom. Barth declares: "To the man who persistently tries to change the truth into untruth, God does not owe eternal patience and . . . deliverance."[8] Yet he maintains that we can sincerely hope for a universal final salvation, and we have grounds for such hope because of the promises of Scripture that God is faithful even while men are faithless and that the gifts and call of God are irrevocable (cf. Rom. 12:29; II Tim. 2:13).

It cannot be denied that the logic of Barth's theology leads him in the direction of universalism. He affirms the universal outreach and dominion of God's grace. It is his conviction that "all men and all creation . . . are ordained to be the theatre of His glory and therefore the recipients and bearers of His Word."[9] He also adheres to the irresistibility of the grace of God in the sense that it cannot be ultimately defeated: "And when there comes the hour of the God who acts in Jesus Christ by the Holy Ghost, no aversion, rebellion or resistance on the part of non-Christians will be strong enough to resist the fulfilment of the promise of the Spirit which is pronounced over them too."[10] Indeed, "the stream [of grace] is too strong and the dam too weak for us to be able reasonably to expect anything but the collapse of the dam and the onrush of the waters. In this sense Jesus Christ is the hope even of these non-Christians."[11]

In his view God's predestination of all men to salvation "cannot be overthrown or reversed. Rejection cannot again become the portion or affair of man. . . . There is no condemnation—literally none—for those that are in Christ Jesus."[12] After the coming of Jesus Christ unbelief becomes "an objective, real, ontological impossibility. . . . Faith, however, has become an objective, real ontological inevitability for all, for every man."[13]

In this theology there is no final rejection of men by God, no irrevocable condemnation. Wrath is the penultimate word, but love is the ultimate word (cf.

Isa. 54:8; Mic. 7:18). Yet there is a self-damnation in which man resists and thwarts the love of God, in which he swims against the stream of divine grace. "But if we will what God does not will," Barth says, "we . . . have God against us, and therefore we hurry and run and stumble and fall into eternal perdition." [14] Whether man can persist in his rejection is dubious, however, in the light of Barth's strong emphasis on the sovereignty of grace. Any opposition to what has already been decided and enacted by the living God can only be self-destructive and self-defeating.

Barth sees the world as both redeemed and unredeemed. To understand this paradox we need to be reminded that redemption in its widest sense encompasses man's objective deliverance from the penalty and bondage of sin, his subjective liberation through the work of the Holy Spirit, and his perfection and glorification. [15] In the first meaning redemption is practically equivalent to reconciliation except that the emphasis is on deliverance and liberation rather than the restoration of communion with God. Barth maintains that we and all people already have both "the forgiveness of sins" and "redemption" "through the blood of Christ." [16] When the Holy Spirit acts upon us we become liberated *de facto*. In faith we perceive that "we are redeemed, set free, children of God," though we do not yet see this as "fulfilled and completed." [17] The eschatological redemption or glorification signifies the consummation of redemption and reconciliation:

he sometimes describes it as "full redemption." Redemption has been achieved for us through the victory of Jesus Christ, but it remains invisible or hidden; it has still to be made visible. In his *Church Dogmatics* IV, 3, Barth emphasizes the "not yet" of redemption, whereas previously he had stressed the "already" of reconciliation and salvation, though this note is still very much present. He returns to a decided emphasis on the accomplished work of salvation in his *Church Dogmatics* IV, 4, but he seeks to show how this calls for a response in a life of obedience.

In some places it is clear that Barth sees the cross of Christ as encompassing salvation in its totality. There is fulfilled in the cross of Christ, he says, "the mission, the task, and the work of the Son of God: the reconciliation of the world with God. There takes place here the redemptive judgment of God on all men." [18] In Jesus Christ "God wills to magnify and does in fact magnify His own glory . . . to the inclusion of the redemption and salvation of the world." [19] Because of our certainty that Christ has "achieved our reconciliation . . . we can be 'so much more' sure that He has achieved our salvation as well." [20] And again: "All healing, all cleansing, all victory over death and the devil, are now to be regarded and believed and proclaimed as accomplished in Him." [21]

Robert Macafee Brown and Ian Fraser in their stress on the all-encompassing victory of Christ definitely reflect Barth's position, but they tend to go further in seeing the warfare with the powers of darkness as virtually if not actually concluded. In their view the world "already is redeemed," and all that remains is a mopping-up operation.[22] Barth also occasionally speaks in this fashion,[23] but he nevertheless maintains that light must still battle with darkness and that the warfare is not consummated, though the outcome is guaranteed and the victory is secured. To be sure, this is not a battle between equals, since the foe has been radically defeated, but even in his irrevocable defeat and virtual collapse he is able to spread fear and doubt among people. His power has been taken from him, his kingdom is no more, but he still has the capability to deceive.[24] This is why Barth can at times portray mankind as liberated and redeemed in actuality and then again as redeemed only in principle and not in fact. There is an "already" but also a "not yet" in Barth's doctrine of salvation. Now we live in the realm of grace; but the realm of glory, where sin and death no longer exist, is still to be revealed. We are redeemed in hope in that we do not yet possess the fruits of our redemption.

The eschaton is anticipated now in the knowledge of our salvation, but it will be ushered in its consummated fullness in a climactic event that will bring down the curtain on world history. Then the city of man will become the eternal city of God. Then the kingdom of nature, which even in its sin and corruption is illumined by grace, will be transfigured into the kingdom of glory. Then the new heaven and the new earth, which already exist in the mind of God, will become visible to the whole creation. At that time too the new reality present in the resurrection of Jesus Christ will encompass and transform the totality of the human race, which is even now included by divine fiat in this new reality. Whether men even in their resistance and contumacy can stand against this final revelation of God's grace and glory is highly problematical in the context of Barth's theology.

According to Barth redemption was already begun in creation, for creation was a redemptive event. In his act of creation God shows himself as "Lord" and "Victor" over the chaos. Yet redemption needs to be realized and fulfilled in the work of reconciliation. Its perfect realization and revelation are still ahead of us. This "future salvation" of the world is "the fruit of its reconciliation."[25] At the same time the eschatological redemption is already present in the resurrection of Jesus Christ. Christ has achieved our redemption as well as our reconciliation,[26] but this great fact needs to be made manifest.

While Barth maintains that creation is the presupposition of reconciliation and redemption, he contends that in another sense reconciliation is prior to creation in that it has already happened in the preexistence of Jesus Christ. The Eternal Son of God in his determination to unite himself with humanity even before the creation and incarnation already assured our reconciliation and redemption (cf. II Tim. 1:9; Rev. 13:8 KJV). The creation signifies the beginning of the revelation of the eternal decision of reconciliation and redemption which is universal and all-inclusive in its scope. This eternal decision is given historical confirmation and concreteness in the sacrificial life and death of Jesus Christ. In the cross of Christ we see the divine verdict of election and salvation, which is pronounced on all, though not all have been awakened to its far-reaching cosmic significance.

It is interesting to compare Calvin and Barth on this subject. Calvin too sees Christ as the Mediator even before his condescension in human form. He too sees Jesus Christ as containing within himself everything that will be ours in a future redemption. He too believes that Christ had accomplished everything necessary for our salvation, that his sacrifice was definitive and complete. He can even declare that in the death of Christ we have "the complete fulfillment of salvation" and that we "have been born anew" through the resurrection of Christ.[27] Both theologians understand divine election to precede the decision of faith and even the fall of man; yet Calvin is more emphatic than Barth that God's electing grace will invariably give rise to faith. In Calvin's view those who benefit from the election and atonement of Christ are the elect people of God, the community of the faithful. For Barth the benefits of the atonement extend to all, though not all apprehend and perceive. For Calvin, Christ is the mediator of the eternal decree of election; whereas for Barth, Christ is both the Elector and the Elected

One, who includes within himself the totality of mankind. For Calvin, predestination realizes its goal only in the response of faith; whereas for Barth, predestination has reached its goal in Jesus Christ, though its reality and efficacy are not yet manifest in all those who belong to him. For Calvin, personal faith is the instrument or means by which divine election and justification are effected in the lives of men; for Barth, faith is more properly a revelatory sign and consequence of our election and salvation. Although Calvin seeks to make predestination correlative with faith, both men betray a decidedly objectivistic bent, since the decree of predestination is enacted and completed in the eternal counsel of God, though they both insist that what has been decreed must be worked out and made manifest in history. Barth in trying to underline the dynamic character of predestination can even say that though it is a "completed work . . . it is not an exhausted work, a work which is behind us. On the contrary, it is a work which still takes place in all its fullness today."[28]

While both theologians maintain that the Christian can have assurance of his election and salvation, Barth's position that we can be certain only of Christ's faithfulness to us but not of our faithfulness to Christ tends to conflict with the Calvinist doctrine of eternal security. Barth would never say, however, that people can fall out of the sphere of God's grace and goodness, though he does affirm the ever-present but incomprehensible possibility of falling away from the path marked out by grace.

The crucial difference between the two men is that Calvin adheres to particular election and redemption while Barth affirms the universality and all-inclusiveness of the electing and reconciling work of God. The doctrine of "limited atonement," a hallmark of Calvinist orthodoxy, is definitely contradicted by Barth, and here can be seen his affinity to Luther and Wesley. In Calvin all is of grace, but grace is not for all. In Luther and Wesley all is of grace and grace is for all, but not all are for grace. In Barth grace is the source of all creaturely being and goes out to all, but every man is set against grace. Yet every man is caught up in the movement of grace even in the case where there is continued opposition to Christ. At the same time those who defy grace are claimed by grace and remain objects of grace despite their contumacy and folly. The act of turning away from grace is for Barth impossible and it would seem an impermanent condition, since no man can escape from or overturn the all-embracing love and grace of a sovereign God.

It can perhaps be argued that Barth transcends the polarity between universalism and particularism in that he denies both of these as rational principles or even as necessary conclusions of faith. He sees the truth in universalism in that Christ's victory over the chaos is all-encompassing and his love goes out to all. But he also recognizes an element of truth in particularism in that not all open their hearts to

God's love revealed in Jesus Christ, not all receive the message of salvation through the sacrificial death of Christ. Regarding the final destiny of those who persist in saying no to the divine yes, Barth at least at times appears to be noncommittal. At the same time he is unequivocal that the divine yes cannot be finally defeated or thwarted. One thing is certain: we must regard even the non-Christian with a certain degree of optimism, since we know that he too is in the hands of the living God, whose essence is love.

VI

Two Conflicting
Orientations

Karl Barth is a child of both the Reformation and the Enlightenment (*Aufklärung*), and this perhaps accounts for certain seeming inconsistencies in his thought. Without doubt he seeks to stand in the tradition of the Reformation and speak as a Reformed theologian. Indeed, it can even be said that he is an evangelical catholic theologian, since he appeals to Anselm in his methodology and is very close to Augustine in his theory of evil as well as in his conception of freedom. He even has kind words for Thomas Aquinas in his discussion of the perfections of God and predestination.

While the Reformation element is dominant, a perceptive critic of Barth can also discern a marked influence of the Enlightenment, particularly as this is communicated through Schleiermacher and Kant. Platonism, which made a comeback in the early Enlightenment, is also evident in Barth's thinking (especially the earlier Barth), as it is in Schleiermacher's.[1] Both Schleiermacher and Kant sought to overcome the Enlightenment, and Barth followed them in this regard; but like them he did not wholly succeed in breaking free from its spell.[2] In reacting against the Enlightenment he unwittingly adopted some of its themes and concerns. He perceived the hubris that characterized the eighteenth-century Enlightenment but nevertheless regarded this period as still a "Christian century." The cautious admiration that he had for Kant continued into his later years, when he became ever more critical of the intrusion of philosophy into theology. He was able to recommend Kant's treatise on the Enlightenment as a work of enduring value.[3] He even looked forward to a new age of Enlightenment in its best sense in which the music of Mozart and the poetry of Goethe would be received with sensitive ears and open hearts.

Barth's stress on the goodness and harmony of the creation has a definite affinity with the Enlightenment, though he seeks to ground this in Scripture and not human speculation. In contrast to Augustine, Calvin, and Luther, Barth sees this world not as the domain of the devil but as the realm of grace. His preference for Mozart over other noted musicians reflects his conviction that this world is essentially harmonious, orderly, and good.[4] Mozart saw the whole world enveloped in light, and the shadow over creation does not obstruct but instead accentuates this light; indeed light breaks forth from this shadow.[5] The Reformers on the other hand underlined the continuing antithesis between light and darkness, the Holy and the profane, the church and the world. Barth appreciates Mozart because he "heard the negative only in and with the positive."[6] The concept of preestablished harmony was fashionable among some Enlightenment philosophers, and Barth accepts this but gives it a christological basis. With Leibniz he is willing to affirm that this world is "the best of all possible worlds"; yet for Barth this is true only because it has been redeemed by Jesus Christ.[7]

In Barth's theology reconciliation is none other than the renewal and fulfillment of creation. "Reconciliation in Christ," he says, "is the restoration of the lost promise. It renews the status of the creation with its great 'Yes' to man, with its reasonableness of reason."[8] Barth will not say with Schleiermacher, however, that reconciliation is simply the completion of creation.

This brings us to Barth's respect for clear thinking and rationality. Though he maintains that reason in and of itself cannot perceive the truth of faith, when it is enlightened by the Spirit it is then enabled to understand, since the message of the gospel is a rational message. Revelation does not lift man above reason but instead restores reason to its true foundation in the Word of God. Faith connotes the illumination of reason, not a venture into the darkness (as in Luther).[9] The new birth means that man "finally comes to himself, to rationality, to perception of what he was in the counsel of God . . . even before he himself was aware of it."[10] Barth acknowledges that he has "great trust in reason," since it is "a good gift of God." It is helpful in clarifying faith, but it must not be made "the abstract judge of all," for "that is unreasonable." [11]

According to Barth the gospel calls men to become what they already are—sons of God by virtue of their creation in the image of Christ and redemption through the atonement of Christ. The gospel summons man to act in accordance with the law of his own being, and here we see the use of Kantian imagery, though for Barth this law is personified and revealed in Jesus Christ.

While Barth is indubitably closer to Luther and Calvin than to Kant in his overall perspective, he, like Kant, sees freedom as the essential characteristic of man. Luther on the contrary regards bondage as the primary hallmark of the natural man. For Kant freedom is the determination of the will by the moral law. For Barth freedom is self-determination under the total determination of the summons of God. [12] While Kant sees freedom as being always accessible to man despite the existence of an internal, radical evil, Barth recognizes that our freedom needs to be renewed and liberated by Christ. [13] It is Jesus Christ who restores, confirms, and reveals the freedom that is already ours by creation.

Barth's preference for common sense over mystical and ecstatic experience is another indication of his Enlightenment roots. Faith can bring us to a true perception of God, but common sense enables us to live and cope in the world. Common sense with its "rules and inevitabilities and generalisations" is part of the revelation of the wisdom of God. [14] It bears witness to the truth that God is a God of peace, not disorder.

To be sure, Barth denies the validity of a natural knowledge of God. At the same time he insists that all people by virtue of being in Christ have an awareness of the love and gracious presence of God. What Barth denies with the one hand he seems to accept with the other. We cannot on our own come to a true knowledge of God, but we have access to a general knowledge of divine reality given by the universal Christ. This is made evident in the following remark:

On the one hand, our question as to what the Bible offers is an idle one, for we already *have* the answer: all the knowledge that we possess takes its start from the knowledge of God. We are not outside, as it were, but inside. The knowledge of God is not a possibility which we may, or at worst may *not*, apply in our search for a meaning of the world; it is rather the presupposition on the basis of which . . . all our searchings for meaning are made.[15]

While the Enlightenment holds that every man is in touch with the Infinite by virtue of his created being and natural powers, Barth maintains that every man is grasped by the Infinite by virtue of the universal and all-encompassing grace of Christ. Barth's position is here very close to that of Karl Rahner, who also has one foot in the Enlightenment. Indeed, it can be shown that Rahner, with his concept of the "anonymous Christian," one who

manifests Christ's love without conscious faith in
him, is much more than Barth a child of the modern
age.

Though not basing his ethics on "natural and
spiritual laws," Barth nevertheless acknowledges
the validity of such laws on their own level. They are
not the basis of our existence and do not reveal
anything of God as Creator and Lord, but they are
"forms" of the nature of our existence. They indicate
not the reality or substance of the created world but
only the manner of its existence.[16] As is well-known,
natural law figured very highly in the Enlightenment.

Barth's monistic orientation is also closer to that of
the Enlightenment than to the Reformation, which
was much more dualistic. Luther envisioned a
dichotomy between the kingdom of God and the
kingdom of the world, the law and the gospel, grace
and nature. For Barth, on the other hand, there is
only the one eternal kingdom to which all people
belong. The "shadow kingdom" of the devil does not
exist in juxtaposition to the kingdom of God, but as
something that is already behind us and all people,
something that has been "objectively put away." [17]
While the Nothingness "still is in the world, it is in
virtue of the blindness of our eyes and the cover
which is still over us, obscuring the prospect of the
kingdom of God already established as the only
kingdom undisputed by evil." [18] The devil is not an
angelic adversary of God (as in Luther and Calvin)[19]
but an anarchic force within this world which in the

light of Jesus Christ now becomes an instrument of God's will and purpose. Grace moreover signifies the restoration and fulfillment of nature, for man is by nature good, not evil. The "real man" is not corrupted but hidden by sin. The Spirit of Christ reveals to man his true being, which is his being in Christ.

Von Balthasar accuses Barth, especially the early Barth, of theopanism, since it seems that Christ is everywhere present, that his grace encompasses all things and all people. Barth in his earlier phase could even say that "everything natural is holy by that very fact because the Holy, too, is natural."[20] Von Balthasar goes so far as to contend that "Barth is in agreement with the final outlook of Schleiermacher" because of his view that the Word of God "illumines all" and does not shine down simply on a select group of the faithful.[21]

Helmut Thielicke, Paul Althaus, Bernard Ramm, A. D. R. Polman, and some others have fastened the label of "Christomonism" on Barth,[22] though he himself repudiates this designation and not without some justification, since he seeks to be solidly trinitarian. While he makes Christ central, he does not identify Christ with the Godhead. Moreover, he begins not with the timeless idea of Christ but with the Eternal decision to save men in Jesus Christ. At the same time by viewing Christ as the Elector and not simply as the Mediator of election, he tends to blur the distinctions between God the Father and God the Son. By making the kingship of Jesus Christ coterminous with the universal hegemony of Jehovah, he again seems to render these distinctions within the Godhead superfluous.

Barth's this-worldly optimism stands in noticeable contrast to the pessimism of the Reformation, but it does have a marked affinity to the rosier outlook of the Enlightenment. He definitely diverges from the Reformation in his affirmation of the fundamental goodness and Christ-likeness of man. Despite the fall man "has not lost—even in part—the good nature which was created by God, to acquire instead another and evil nature."[23] He boldly propounds that "the human spirit is naturally Christian"[24] and that "what is *Christian* is secretly but fundamentally identical with what is *universally human.*"[25] Compare this with Luther's remark: "No one is by nature Christian or righteous, but altogether sinful and wicked."[26] In Reformation theology the very essence of man is corrupted, though not destroyed, by sin, the *imago Dei* is utterly defaced; and man after the fall can only be considered an enemy of God and Christ.

Barth acknowledges that one of the hallmarks of Enlightenment thought is that "the Christian spirit is identical with the truly humane spirit,"[27] though he challenges this notion in its Enlightenment context because it is associated with the idea of man's autonomy, his independence from God. It is significant, however, that he pays tribute to the eighteenth century for impressing on the consciousness of the church "the truth of the identity of fallen man with the man originally created by God." [28] For Barth the universally human is identical with the truly Christian only because man's humanity is created and sustained in the image of God as revealed in Jesus Christ and every man is a beneficiary of the grace of Christ.[29] In Barth's view man is "from the very outset . . . 'in the Word of God.'"[30]

In this theology, as in the Enlightenment, all people are children of God, all are indissolubly linked to the Eternal, all have been accepted into the family of God. There are no longer any outsiders; all are insiders, since all are in Christ, all are recipients of his love. This indeed palpably conflicts with Calvin's view: "For Scripture everywhere cries aloud, that all are lost; and every man's own conscience bitterly accuses him."[31] It should be recognized, however, that in Barth's theology although man is ontologically and objectively redeemed in Christ, he is nonetheless existentially unredeemed insofar as he lacks the knowledge of his accomplished salvation.

Barth's optimism, to be sure, is grounded in the grace of God, not in the natural resources of man, as with the Enlightenment. While the Enlightenment speaks of man's fulfillment and happiness on the basis of his freedom, Barth refers to man's liberty in service on the basis of his incorporation in Christ. As he expressed it: "To be able to believe, to love and to hope is man's destiny as seen in the light of God's revelation. In Christ it is true and valid for every human being."[32]

In stark contrast to the Reformation and in surprising concord with the Enlightenment Barth endorses "the will for life" and even "the will for power."[33] For Barth self-affirmation is an act of obedience to God. Man must not neglect his natural resources and strengths but use them in the service of his neighbor. Of course, he recognizes the sinful misuse of one's natural powers, the attempt to dominate and control others, but this is no longer the legitimate expression of one's nature but its perversion. While he sees a place for the celebration of life as given by God, the medieval theologians and Reformers put the accent on self-denial, bearing the cross, and the mortification of the flesh. Barth on the contrary maintains that man is not "something that must be overcome" (Nietzsche's caricature of historical Christianity), but instead "that creature destined by God to be a conqueror."[34] This note, of course, can also be discerned in Paul (Rom. 8:37).

Perhaps Barth represents a healthy corrective to the suppression and negation of self so long practiced in Christianity, but it cannot be denied that he here approaches the Renaissance and Enlightenment. Yet his humanism is theological, not philosophical. He begins with God and then proceeds to man, not vice versa. The elevation and glorification of man are possible only because of the condescension of God in Jesus Christ. Moreover, the qualitative distinction between the Creator and the creature is always maintained in his theology, though in his later writings he generally refrains from referring to God as "the Wholly Other" ("*totaliter aliter*"), one of the trademarks of his dialectical period.

One might also argue that Barth's understanding of the Christian vocation as essentially ethical and secular, in the sense that it is faith at work in the world, including the world of politics and economics, reflects modern rather than medieval or Reformation motifs. Man should not prepare for life in another world but instead manifest a life of authenticity and freedom in this world.[35] Both the rationalists and the Pietists of the Enlightenment were preeminently concerned with the practical life that needs to be changed, and Barth reflects elements of this concern, though he seeks to ground it in God's gracious act of reconciliation in Christ. In his theology the Christian is called to witness to Christ by word and deed, to give a concrete demonstration of his faith before men. Faith is basically cognitive and ethical, rather than soteriological, since it signifies the response to a salvation already achieved and not the realization of salvation. It is not the overtly religious life but the ethical life that absorbs Barth's attention.[36] To be sure, he makes an important place for prayer, but includes it in his section on ethics; it is an act of moral obedience to the divine imperative.[37] Even our baptism is not as such a religious rite but a moral commitment to a life of righteousness. Barth stoutly opposes the traditional view that baptism is a means of grace whereby our sins are forgiven and taken away. In his theology one does not fight for the faith or the Word of God (these defend themselves) or even for one's own salvation; instead one is called to fight for social righteousness, for justice, and equality for all men. Here can be seen the seeds of the theologies of revolution and liberation.

Barth joins the Enlightenment in affirming that man has an incontestable obligation to serve his fellow humanity and to promote the general welfare, though he sees this as a sign and witness to the grace of Jesus Christ.[38] We no longer have to be concerned about personal salvation because God has taken care of that in Christ. Our calling is not to salvation but to vocation. Yet regarding the motivation and goal of our service, Barth diverges sharply from the Enlightenment. For the latter the motivation for service is the divine command written into the heart of the universe. Service is a moral duty reflecting the categorical imperative within. For Barth the motivation in our service is gratefulness for what God has done for us in Jesus Christ, and the goal of our service is the glorification of God as we know him in Jesus Christ. In his view the ethical or penultimate springs from the spiritual or ultimate and is directed to it.

Some Enlightenment philosophers advocated a spirit of reverence toward God as the Supreme Being or the Author of nature and submisssion to the divine will. At first sight this might not appear contradictory to Barth's view, but closer examination reveals it to be a far cry from Barth's emphasis on giving glory to the living, personal God who identifies himself with our trials and tribulations in Jesus Christ. In the prevailing strand of the Enlightenment there is no place for confession of sin, petitionary prayer, or biblical proclamation, whereas these are of the very essence of Barth's theology of worship.

In the Enlightenment the sacraments became ordinances of the church. The stress was on the dedication and faithfulness of the subject rather than on the prevenient redemptive grace of God. In Barth's theology Holy Communion becomes a fellowship meal celebrated in the name and for the sake of Christ.[39] It is essentially an ethical response to Christ's death. Baptism is no longer a work of salvation or even the revelation of this salvation but an act of faith and obedience. This viewpoint was anticipated to some extent by Zwingli and also the Anabaptists, but it began to make real inroads into the mainstream of Protestantism in the eighteenth and nineteenth centuries. The church itself is regarded not as a unique means of grace, as an agent of salvation, but as a fellowship of believers gathered to hear the Word of God. The church is a sign and witness to the salvation that has already been accomplished for all humankind. Barth sees the church not as our "Holy Mother" out of which faith comes, but as the earthen vessel in which faith shines.[40] What distinguishes the church from the world is that the former knows of its salvation. The world, which is in effect the invisible church, still awaits the revelation of the work of reconciliation and redemption perfected in Jesus Christ.

Barth's stricture on mysticism, which has already been alluded to, likewise points to an affinity with the Enlightenment. There are ineradicable points of conflict between the tradition of Christian mysticism and the theology of the Reformers, but at the same time they sought to maintain the mystical dimension of the faith. Luther at one place described faith as a rapture by which man is lifted above himself into God, and Calvin referred to a mystical communion between the indwelling Christ and the believer. For Barth salvation is not so much mystical experience as humanization, the realization and restoration of man's true humanity. Revelation is not the fulfillment or culmination of man's religious quest but its negation and abolition. In his emphasis on the ethical over the mystical Barth stands closer to Ritschl and Kant than to Schleiermacher. The ethical and mystical dimensions of the faith were both very much present in the main-line theology of the Reformation.

Barth's concept of the ministry may also reflect the secularization process associated with the Renaissance and continuing into the Enlightenment, though here we must be cautious since his position has some biblical warrant. While criticizing Calvin's conception of the ministry as "exclusive" and "aristocratic," Barth praises the Pietists of the seventeenth and eighteenth centuries for rediscovering and giving tangible expression to the New

Testament concept of the priesthood of all believers. With many of the rationalists as well as the Protestant sectarians Barth regards sacerdotalism as a curse that has plagued the institutional church for centuries. "In the age of the Enlightenment," he remarks, "a new impulse was given to the emancipation of the laity by the gradual but inexorable development of a general freedom of faith and conscience."[41] For him every Christian is a minister by virtue of his ordination into full-time kingdom service at his baptism. Every Christian is "called" to embark upon an apostolic vocation, to share in the prophetic and priestly ministry of Christ. Every Christian is endowed with spiritual gifts that enable him to bear witness to his faith and minister to others; yet Barth recognizes that not all are equipped to conduct public worship and to preach publicly. He seeks to ground his concept of the ministry in the New Testament, and he is able to build a persuasive case, but he nevertheless reflects the sectarian and Enlightenment suspicion of holy orders and sacraments. He questions the validity of a special ministry of the Word and sacraments understood as a divinely instituted separate office in the church.[42] Barth like Kant and Schleiermacher as well as the radical Pietists strives to overcome the traditional distinctions between clergy and laity.

This ambivalent relation to the Reformation is also apparent in Barth's reservations concerning the concept of the supernatural, though the Reformers would stand with him in his attacks upon the world of magic and superstition. His this-worldly concern in which the vision of a transfigured or perfected world figures more prominently than a supernatural heaven reveals him to be more modern than Reformed.[43] He acknowledges that the Christian hope must contain some element of chiliasm,[44] and in his earlier writings he made occasional references to a coming millennium. His concept of the communion of saints as the cherished memory of the departed in the present consciousness of the church as over against spiritual intercourse between the departed in glory and the saints on earth is still another indication of his break with a Reformed and also Catholic way of thinking.

Yet though Barth has an aversion to the term "supernatural" because of its peculiar associations with both Thomism and fundamentalism, Wieman and Meland are indubitably correct in categorizing Barth as a "neo-supernaturalist," since he affirms a God who infinitely transcends nature and history.[45] He is also a supernaturalist in his affirmation of the invisible world of angels, who play a significant role in his doctrine of creation. Surely one should not overlook his incontestable adherence to the Virgin Birth of Christ and the bodily resurrection of our Lord, though he does not use these for purposes of validating the claims of the faith before the world as do the fundamentalists.

While Barth is naturally not kindly disposed toward skepticism and secularism, it is manifestly clear that he does not consider these nearly as baneful as religious fanaticism, syncretistic mysticism, and occultism.[46] Religiosity, not secularity, is the principal foe of the gospel. He reminds us that the polemic of the Bible is directed "not against the godless world but against the *religious* world."[47] Unreligious men such as Kant and Overbeck have felt the importance and gravity of the question of God more keenly than the zealously pious. What makes the secularistic mentality dangerous is that it often assumes the form of a covert religion and also opens the door to false religions.

Unbelief in the sense of open atheism is to be deplored, but it need not be an occasion for alarm, since the unbeliever may be understandably disenchanted by the pretensions and hypocrisy of organized religion.[48] In the western world he is often reacting against the misunderstandings prevailing in Christian theology (as with Feuerbach and Nietzsche) or injustices tolerated by the church (as with Marx). It should also be borne in mind that since every man is a hearer of the Word of God, "the unbelief of the sinner," as von Balthasar says in interpreting Barth, "can be nothing but a vain, already quashed rebellion against the truth of God within him."[49] This is why unbelief cannot be taken as seriously as in the writings of some frenetic apologists. Superstition, which is a false reasoning that gives birth to fear, is worse than atheism, which is reason deceived. It is possible to enter into dialogue with honest atheists, particularly those who are motivated by social concern, since the broken social visions of man are fulfilled in the kingdom of God. Barth does not share the Enlightenment vision of an open world of continuous dialogue, since man cannot come to faith by dialogue, though he can advance the cause of social justice in this way. Barth's criticism of the Second Vatican Council is that it put too much emphasis on dialogue and not enough on proclamation. Barth was nevertheless a firm supporter of the Christian-Marxist dialogue, though he spurned any kind of rapprochement with National Socialism, which in his mind signified a demonic religion.[50]

Barth's acceptance of the historical-critical method in the treatment of Scriptures, a product of the Enlightenment, may also indicate a departure from the Reformation. Yet one must be cautious here, for Barth thinks of the Bible not only as a human witness to revelation but as revelation itself mediated through human words.[51] Historical criticism can only throw light upon the historical and cultural background of the text: it cannot give us its theological and spiritual significance. Barth remains true to the Reformation in his view that it is the Holy Spirit alone who enables the believer to perceive and hear the real Word of God that is both embodied and hidden in the scriptural text. He acknowledges that Scripture is humanly fallible as well as divinely infallible, but his judgment on the fallibility of Scripture is a theological, not a cultural or scientific one. Barth makes an attempt to show that it has its roots in the scriptural witness itself and not in secular historical criticism. His understanding of inspiration as pertaining more to the writers than to the text shows the influence of Pietism.

Finally it might be well to consider the criticism leveled at Barth by some Evangelicals that he subordinates God's holiness to his love. Bernard Ramm has accused Barth of a love monism.[52] Barth declares: "God's being is His loving. He is all that He is as the One who loves. All His perfections are the perfections of His love."[53] And again: "We are not . . . making any crucial change of theme when we go on to speak of God's holiness. We are merely continuing to speak of God's grace."[54] Barth does acknowledge that God's love is informed by his holiness and that his holiness must never be separated from his love. Yet he does not always appear to see the tension between the two. God's wrath is considered a form of his love more than a reaction of his holiness to man's sin, and in this way Barth fails to acknowledge the tension and even the conflict between God's love and his wrath. It is well to remember that the Enlightenment theologians and philosophers rejected the idea of the wrath of God as a throwback to primitive religion and thought of God only in terms of his love. This was also true of Schleiermacher and Ritschl, who stand in basic though sometimes broken continuity with the Enlightenment, especially in its later phases.[55] To Barth's credit he does try to take seriously the biblical witness concerning the wrath of God and thereby makes a place for the concepts of satisfaction and expiation in his doctrine of the atonement. At the same time he rejects the historical Protestant view that God is love only in Christ and that outside of Christ he is basically wrath. He also takes issue with the Reformation idea of a secret will of God, which is informed by God's majesty and holiness, and his revealed will, which is love. For Barth, God is in his essence love and grace, and his holiness and wrath are forms of his love. I prefer to say that God is in his essence both holiness and love and that his wrath is an expression of both of these together. My position is close to Barth's at this point but not the very same. It should be kept in mind that he sees the atonement of Christ not only as a demonstration of the "pure mercy" of God but also as the vindication of his "perfect righteousness."[56]

In this discussion it is well to recognize that Barth stands much more firmly in the heritage of the Reformation than in that of the Enlightenment. His acceptance of the universality and radicality of sin in the life of man marks him as a Reformed theologian. To be sure, he describes sin as an "ontological impossibility," as something that is alien to rather than inherent in the nature of man, but he nevertheless insists that it happens and that it corrupts every aspect of man's existence. He affirms the bondage of the will and the sinful distortion of man's reasoning, though he is adamant that sin does not alter the essential being of man. Man's true nature, even though marred and obscured by sin, still reflects the glory of its Creator. Sin is inhuman and unnatural rather than human and natural, and though it is a blot upon man's nature it can never displace this nature.

His determined opposition to the Enlightenment concepts of the inevitability of progress and the inherent perfectibility of man reveal the wide gulf as well as the continuity between his theology and that great intellectual and cultural movement of modern times. At the same time Barth does contend that in Christ man can be made perfect and that the whole world is moving toward a final redemption. He, of course, recognizes that because of sin man never remains totally in Christ, but he seems to regard perfection in Christ as a possibility given by grace.[57]

Man must never confuse any cultural break-through to greater human freedom with the kingdom of God, but the Spirit of God will indeed be working in man's strides toward greater justice and equality, and we should see these as signs and parables of the coming kingdom of God. "The Church," he says, "will not see the coming of the kingdom of God in any human cultural achievement, but it will be alert for the signs which, perhaps in many cultural achievements, announce that the kingdom approaches."[58] We should try to discern not only the Word of God in the Bible but also the signs of the times in the light of the biblical revelation. The Spirit of God is at work in universal history as well as in biblical history, but we can apprehend his working in the former only in the light of the latter.

Barth's unflinching affirmation of the sole mediation of Jesus Christ also attests his credentials as a theologian in the tradition of the Reformation. For Kant, Jesus was simply a "teacher of the gospel" or the "founder of the church." The object of our faith is the ideal of moral perfection that was exemplified in Jesus to a high degree but that must also be exemplified in us. Ritschl, who leaned heavily upon Kant, saw Jesus as the bearer of an ethical-religious ideal. For Hegel, in whom the Enlightenment resurfaces, Jesus typifies the perfect realization of divine-human unity to which all men approximate. Barth on the contrary is adamant that Jesus is God Incarnate, the divine Savior from sin, apart from whose sacrificial death and glorious resurrection no man can be saved. Yet he does not deny that non-Christians too are included in the history of salvation,[59] and that the grace of Christ reaches out to all men irrespective of their belief or unbelief. Like Reinhold Niebuhr he alludes to a hidden presence of Christ in the world outside the church, though he does not develop this theme to any considerable degree. Also in agreement with Niebuhr he opposes missions to the Jews on the grounds that they too belong to the biblical covenant of grace, though they have not yet recognized that Jesus Christ is the One who fulfills this covenant.[60]

His fervent contention that the truth of faith is knowable only through divine revelation again sharply distinguishes Barth's theology from the world- and life-view of the Enlightenment. He stands with the Reformers in his perception that the truth of the gospel is simply not available to human reason. He asserts that "not at any time nor in any respect can any who will, reach out and take it."[61] Barth contends against both the Enlightenment and the nineteenth-century liberal theology that was its heir that faith is a divine but not a human possibility. God can be known only through his Word and Spirit, but when the Spirit acts upon man as he is confronted with the gospel he then truly knows the living God and his plan and purpose for the world. Such a position definitely conflicts with Pannenberg's espousal of "the open rationality of the Enlightenment," the view that revelation is "open to general reasonableness."[62]

The kerygmatic orientation of Barth's theology also contrasts with the apologetic orientation of the theology of the Enlightenment. Rationalistic apologetics dominated the scene during the later seventeenth and eighteenth centuries. Even those of a more orthodox persuasion sought to defend the faith at the bar of reason and thereby paid homage to the one authority acknowledged by the secular philosophers of the Enlightenment. Barth's opposition to natural theology made it impossible for him to be in any way sympathetic to the elaborate proofs for the existence of God and the immortality of the soul that were fashionable in that period. At the same time Barth believed that it is possible to demonstrate the existence of God to the faithful, as did Anselm, but this is not a natural proof but a compelling witness given by faith to faith.[63]

Unlike the theologians of the Enlightenment as well as the mediating theologians of his own day, including Brunner and Tillich, Barth maintains that we are to ignore the fact that our hearers may be unbelievers.[64] We are not to seek for common ground because we already stand on common ground. This is not by virtue of any innate capacity within man to hear and respond to the gospel but because both Christian and non-Christian have the "image of God," a gift that neither controls. The *imago Dei* is a relationship with God by which man exists as a human being. Sin impairs but cannot sunder this relationship. We need not be defensive or apologetic in our proclamation, since what we proclaim answers the deepest yearnings of man and speaks to his true being, which is his being in Christ.

Barth's reservations concerning the capacity of reason to perceive divine truth were not entirely absent from the Enlightenment. The Enlightenment too, especially in its later stages, sought to acknowledge the limits of reason, and this was particularly evident in Hume and Kant.[65] It was even recognized that there are certain mysteries that cannot be penetrated by rational inquiry. It has been said that the Enlightenment stressed not so much the omnipotence of reason as the omnicompetence of criticism.[66] The general stance of the philosophers of the later Enlightenment was a naturalistic empiricism, and Barth definitely shared their distrust of speculative metaphysics and their strictures on moral and philosophical absolutes,[67] for such are the product of the vanity of reason. Yet he would take issue with a purely empirical methodology as well as a rationalistic one, since the Word of God is hidden from sight as well as understanding and can be known only as he gives himself to be known in his self-revelation.

While Kant and Hume sought to affirm the limitations of reason on the basis of reason, Barth propounded the limits of its outreach on the basis of divine revelation. Kant's expressed aim was to point out the boundary of knowledge in order to make room for faith; Barth on the other hand was able to discern this boundary in the light of faith.

Barth's conception of revelation as historical definitely conflicts with the Enlightenment stress on eternal truths. For Lessing the accidental truths of history can never become the proof of necessary truths of reason. Yet the early Barth underplayed the historical character of revelation and spoke of Eternity breaking into time but never actually entering the historical process. The finite is not capable of receiving the infinite (*finitum non capax infiniti*), and therefore man must fix his gaze beyond the confines of space and time. The Moment of revelation, he said, is always wholly new; it has no continuity with the before and after. The incarnation was depicted as occurring in superhistory or prehistory (*Urgeschichte*).[68] Sometimes the impression is given that revelation was less a historical event than a demonstration of an eternal truth of which man was ignorant, viz., that God has overcome sin in himself from all eternity. The "event" did not really change things. At the same time as his theology progressed, Barth became ever more conscious of the significance of revelation in history and became steadily more futuristic in his thinking. The coming of Christ was described no longer in terms of the fulfillment of time in Eternity but of the Eternal One meeting us in the future as he has come to us in the past. Barth could even speak of God as having time and history within himself.

There are other areas of disagreement between Barth and the Enlightenment: his affirmation of the living, active God who intervenes in history over the deistic or idealistic God who remains aloof from history; his stout defense of the Trinity as opposed to the God of an abstract monotheism or an impersonal pantheism; his recognition of the mystery and paradox in faith; and his firm commitment to *sola gratia*, that salvation is by grace and not by works. Moreover, Barth's appeal is not to the categorical imperative within, the immanent moral law, natural conscience, but to the "Commander," the living Lord of history whose will alone is the perfect good. One should bear in mind that Barth stands much closer to the so-called "Christian Enlightenment" than to the Enlightenment proper, and in the former personal faith in Jesus Christ and a recognition of his incomparable grace are still retained.[69]

While the Enlightenment envisioned a cosmopolitan brotherhood that would give corporate identity to the universal truth that all men are brothers, Barth proclaimed the coming of the kingdom of God that would make visible the brotherhood of all men in Christ. For Barth men are brothers not by virtue of their common humanity as such (the Enlightenment view) but because of their universal participation in Christ, the true Man. Moreover, the kingdom of God will not simply bind men together in brotherhood but will unite them in the service of the glory of God. And this kingdom is wholly a gift of God, not a work of man.

For the Enlightenment there is a pathway from man to God. In Barth's theology this man is Jesus Christ. Barth begins not with God in himself but with the God-Man; this is why he says that his approach is "theoanthropocentric" rather than simply theocentric, since it takes for its point of departure the Word that has become flesh (John 1:14).[70] Yet Jesus Christ is to be understood not only as the God who becomes man but also as the man who is exalted to God. The atonement signifies not only "a movement from above to below," from God to man, but also "a movement from below to above, the movement of reconciled man to God."[71] In contrast to all humanistic religion, however, Barth insists that the latter movement is contingent on the former.

In this discussion it must not be supposed that the Enlightenment was wholly in error and the Reformation totally in the right. Certainly the Enlightenment was superior to the Reformation and closer to the real spirit of Christianity in its demand for the toleration of religious minorities.[72] Nor do I wish to imply that whenever Barth appears to break with the

Reformation this means that he must therefore be moving in the thought forms and spirit of the Enlightenment. It can be shown at many significant places that Barth has come to some of his startling conclusions through a fresh wrestling with Scripture. I maintain, however, that Barth was unwittingly influenced by the Enlightenment particularly through the intellectual giants with whom he had to contend in his theological education, especially Kant, Schleiermacher, Harnack, and Hermann.[73] At the same time, unless Barth had been compelled to grapple with the thinking of such men, he would not have been able to amass the formidable intellectual tools by which he succeeded in part in stemming the tide of Neo-Protestantism and presenting a theological alternative that proved to be credible at least to a considerable segment of the church.

I believe that Barth's inveterate biblical orientation is very much evident in his trenchant criticism of certain traditional Protestant notions—that man is reduced to nothingness by grace, that the essence of man is sin, and that the mass of the human race is predestined to perdition. It should be recognized, however, that none of these ideas was a guiding motif in the theologies of either Calvin or Luther, though such sentiments were sometimes expressed by the Reformers and even more by certain of their followers.

The Enlightenment signified a vigorous reaction against the world- and life-denying tendencies within historical Christianity, and given the superstition and injustices that the church spawned in the past, much of its reaction was justified. Barth, being a product of modern German education, could not remain unaffected by the legitimate protests and concerns of the philosophers and theologians of the period of the Enlightenment. At the same time, he saw that the dethroning of God can only mean the enthroning of man and that true humanism is only attained when man discovers his humanity in the image of God, not when man tries to become God. According to Barth this true humanism was already very much present in the Holy Bible, and it was rediscovered from time to time in the history of the church. Whether Barth's humanism is in fact a biblical humanism, whether he drew his primary inspiration from the Scriptures, has been questioned, though in my view he is basically a biblical and evangelical theologian. At the same time he is also a child of the modern age, a product of the heritage of the Enlightenment, and in his reaction against it he nevertheless retained certain significant ideas and concerns that stand at variance with the faith of the Reformation. That Barth is less biblical and evangelical because of his indebtedness to the Enlightenment is an open question, but that he cannot be considered a completely faithful and obedient son of the Reformation is probably indisputable. Yet the genius of the Reformed tradition is to be always reformed and not simply to repeat the formulas of past ages, and this Barth has tried to do.

The fact that Barth has appropriated the ideas and

concerns of both the Reformation and the Enlightenment as well as of the pre-Reformation church attests to the catholicity of his vision. Yet he always seeks to give the evangelical message priority and steadfastly resists any attempt to accommodate this message to the spirit of the times (Zeitgeist). Such at least has consistently been his intention, though understandably he could not isolate himself or his message from currents of thought that prevailed in the secular culture of his time or the more distant past. It should be noted too that it is the Christian strand in the Age of Enlightenment (particularly Pietism) that has had the greatest impact upon him.[74]

It may be well to compare Barth and Reinhold Niebuhr at this point. Niebuhr sought consciously to synthesize the Renaissance view of the infinite possibilities of man and the Reformation view of the universality and inevitability of sin. Barth spurned any kind of synthesis with Renaissance or Enlightenment thought and sought to be a thoroughgoing biblical and evangelical theologian. His appeal was mainly to the testimony of Scripture and not to the wisdom of history, which was accepted by Niebuhr as a valid though not indefeasible criterion. The remnants of modern liberalism in Barth's thinking are there not by conscious design but by a kind of unconscious assimilation arising from an attempt to take seriously the challenges to the faith posed by the modern world view.

Barth has rightly contended that theology must

use the language and thought-concepts of philosophy in order to communicate the abiding truth of the gospel but that it must not let itself be ruled by these concepts. Philosophy cannot lay the groundwork for theology (as in Thomas Aquinas), nor are the insights of religion and theology fulfilled in philosophy (as in Hegel). Philosophy should be seen as the pinnacle of natural wisdom, the advocate of man and the world, but therefore also as a potential adversary whose claims when made absolute will invariably conflict with Christian faith.[75] Theology can engage in helpful dialogue with philosophy in order to comprehend better the misunderstandings and failings of the secular culture and in addition to discern the light of the wisdom of the Word of God that is present in the world of unbelief. This is not natural theology but a theology of creation that recognizes that man even in his sin cannot hide the light of Jesus Christ from the eyes of faith. The creative insights and concepts of secular philosophy can be converted or "baptized" into the service of the Word of God by those who have a profound understanding of both Scripture and culture. Yet there is a risk in such an undertaking, the risk that the meaning of the gospel might become confused with the misconceptions of secular thought.

Barth has felt free to utilize concepts derived from Plato, Aristotle, Leibniz, Kant, Hegel, and others, and for the most part he has succeeded in incorporating these concepts into a Christian life- and world-view.

Yet he has not succeeded completely, particularly where philosophical meanings derived from the Enlightenment have given him too rosy a picture of man and the world. Followers of Barth might well reply here that Barth's optimism has biblical warrant, since we are told that God's glory will fill the whole earth (Num. 14:21; Hab. 2:14; 3:3; Isa. 11:9; 40:5; Ps. 97:6), and that the grace of Christ was totally triumphant over the forces of evil (John 12:31; Col. 2:15). The reader must judge for himself, but if Barth has gone too far in his exaltation of man and the world, as I think he has, it surely must be attributed to his supreme confidence in the universality and invincibility of God's grace and his heartfelt thankfulness for the riches of God's mercy as revealed in Christ just as much if not considerably more than to any indebtedness to the philosophy of the Enlightenment or its immediate successors. The Enlightenment played a formative role in his theological development, but essentially he moved in the world of biblical faith. Because of his biblical moorings Barth was able to transcend and also sharply challenge the Enlightenment even while standing partly within it. This was not possible for Kant or Schleiermacher, who were swept up in the tide of the intellectual and cultural awakening of their time, though biblical themes were not wholly submerged in their writings and indeed, especially in Schleiermacher, resurfaced now and again.

VII

Barth
in Retrospect

In giving a concluding theological appraisal of Karl Barth's doctrine of salvation, I shall be frank in sharing my reservations, though I shall express them only in the context of a basic appreciation for his overall contribution to evangelical theology. Moreover, the questions that will be raised are to be understood as coming from a student to a theological master rather than from a hostile critic who does not really share the same basic presuppositions of faith.

First, Barth's contention that the key to the atonement lies in the descent of God to man rather than in the sacrifice of man to God signalizes a rediscovery of patristic themes that have persisted in the history of theology, though muted by Anselmian motifs. One must not, of course, discount the manhood of Jesus as necessary for the fulfillment of the legal requirements of God's righteousness, but Barth's point is that the manhood was simply the instrument whereby the living God satisfied the demands of his own holiness. Moreover, God in the person of his Son was motivated to incarnate himself in human flesh and bear man's sin and guilt through his infinite compassion. A gracious God was not simply the outcome of the atonement but its precondition. I agree with Barth that the atonement was efficacious because it was initiated by God and carried through by God, though in the form of man.

I also heartily concur in Barth's concern to maintain the objectivity in Christian salvation. In the subjective view of the atonement men are reconciled to God by a change of attitude, which he effects in them. A full theory of the atonement sees that the death of Christ involves a radical transformation in the human situation. Barth is certainly correct that at Calvary something was decisively accomplished on man's behalf independent of his faith or works (cf. Rom. 3:3, 4; 5:10). The atonement is the presupposition and foundation of both faith and works. Here Barth is in absolute agreement with the Reformation.

Yet Barth tends to go further in seeing the transformation wrought by Christ as something even more radical than the remission of sins and the victory of grace over the powers of darkness. For him the atoning work of Christ effects a total reversal in the life and destiny of man, a complete turning (*Umkehr*) or revolution, in which sin is displaced by righteousness, in which the kingdom of darkness is replaced by the kingdom of light. We appreciate Barth's emphasis on the triumphal aspect of the atonement, but is this triumph so all-embracing that there is no longer a real adversary to God and his kingdom?[1] Again, Barth's concern is with the objective, extrinsic transformation effected in

Christ,[2] but true atonement also involves an inward transformation in the human heart. The atonement of Christ cannot be regarded as complete apart from the change that it effects in the subjective disposition of man.

Despite his varied attempts to qualify his objectivistic stance, it is our contention that Barth does not finally succeed in holding the objective and subjective dimensions of salvation in true dialectical relation. It seems that not only is the objective prior to the subjective but that the real decision has already been "resolved and actually accomplished in the eternal will of God."[3] The historical realization and fulfillment of God's victory over evil has taken place in the life and death of Jesus Christ. In many places Barth speaks of Jesus Christ as embodying both the objective and subjective poles of salvation, though he acknowledges that the benefits and fruits of salvation must also be manifest in the lives of believers. Even the early Barth, who was still heavily influenced by existentialism, could declare: "Christ in you must never be apprehended as a subjective status which will some day be inaugurated and fulfilled: rather, it is an objective status already fulfilled and already established. ... The status is theirs already by the faithfulness of God displayed in the mission of His Son."[4]

Yet we would be doing an injustice to Barth if we portrayed him as exclusively or wholly objectivistic. He takes pains to affirm the necessity for the subjective apprehension and appropriation of what

God has wrought for us in Jesus Christ. Although God's verdict and direction and promise have been pronounced over all, "the hand of God has not touched all in such a way that they can see and hear, perceive and accept and receive all that God is for all and therefore for them."[5] All people participate in the actuality (not merely the possibility) of the obedience of Jesus Christ by the choice of God (de jure); but God's choice may become our own, thereby making our participation in the true obedience of Christ de facto. In a secondary sense the knowledge of salvation may also be considered "an event of salvation."[6] Salvation history includes the human perception, appropriation, and comprehension of the Christ event. Barth refuses to speak of a correlative on man's side to divine revelation and salvation which is a condition for this salvific event, but he does acknowledge the need for a correspondence on man's side to the transformation that has been wrought on his behalf in Jesus Christ.

Yet in the Barthian scheme Jesus Christ is the ontic dimension and faith the noetic dimension of salvation. In Jesus Christ the fullness of the reality of salvation was achieved for men, and the Holy Spirit is the means by which men apprehend this reality. The cross of Christ is the redemptive event, and faith is the perception of this event. Barth does not deny that in the knowledge of the reality of Christ that takes place in faith, man undergoes an ontological change "within the once-for-all ontological condition created for all men by Jesus Christ."[7] The knowledge of salvation in its deepest sense is much more than an intellectual process: it involves an interior change that affects the totality of man's being. At the same time, it reflects or mirrors rather than fulfills the salvation once for all accomplished in the life and death of Christ.

Barth is adamant that the salvation that Christ procured is complete and needs no supplementation. "We need no repetition or realization of our redemption," he insists. "Christ has achieved all of this perfectly, once-for-all! The task of the Church is to announce the good news of the perfect work of Christ done for all."[8] He will not tolerate any suggestion that salvation must be realized or fulfilled in faith; this is the heresy of Pietism. Nor is salvation realized or re-presented in the sacraments; this is the heresy of Catholicism. Because Jesus Christ is the Baptizer, what the priest or pastor does can only point to what has already been done by Christ. Barth acknowledges the decision element in faith, but this decision does not procure salvation but simply ratifies the salvation that Christ has already achieved. In Barth's eyes to contend that God's saving work in Christ needs to be realized or reenacted in human experience connotes that this work was in some way deficient. The work of salvation is completed, though the plan of salvation is still to be consummated in that all have not been confronted by this work.

According to Barth faith signifies inner spiritual renewal as well as cognitive awareness. In faith man begins to reflect his new being in Christ. In this action "there begins and takes place a new and particular being of man."[9] At the same time faith itself is not a cause of salvation, even an instrumental cause, but a response to salvation. It is a participation in the event of salvation but one in which man receives or apprehends what has already been totally effected for him. Gollwitzer describes the role of faith in Barth's theology as "subsequential and non-fundamental."[10] Arnold Come warns against "the emptying of faith" in his analysis of the dangers in Barthianism.[11]

In theologians like Luther and Jonathan Edwards faith is not merely a response or answer to a salvation already achieved but a condition or qualification for the concrete realization of this salvation. Luther declared that it is not enough to say "through Christ": we must also affirm "through faith." It is not possible to be "saved through Christ without doing anything and without having to give any evidence of faith."[12] The "wonderful exchange" whereby our sins become Christ's and his righteousness ours takes place not only in Christ but also in faith. Faith can thus be considered a part of reconciliation itself.[13] For Edwards faith is not a mere instrument (as in much traditional Reformed theology) but "the grand condition of the covenant of Christ, by which we are in Christ."[14] Yet both these theologians insisted that even the act of faith is a work of divine grace within us, and this simply means that the objective work of Christ on the cross and the subjective work of his Spirit within us are correlative. None can believe except those who have been redeemed by Christ at Calvary, but none can be redeemed except those who cling to Christ in faith. The cross of Christ really saves and does not just make salvation possible, but it really saves only those who are crucified and buried with Christ in baptism and faith (Rom. 6:11).[15]

The decisive distinction in Barth's theology is not between the saved and the lost or the elect and the reprobate but between those who know and those who do not know. "Even before he becomes a Christian," Barth says, "he is in continuity with God in Christ, but he has not yet discovered it. He realizes it only when he begins to believe. . . . The distinction is not between redeemed and non-redeemed, but between those who realize it and those who do not."[16]

I agree with Emil Brunner and Arnold Come over Herbert Hartwell that Barth does not succeed in doing justice to the subjective dimension of salvation or in holding both dimensions in balance.[17] The paradox of salvation is ever again sundered in his emphasis on the objective to the detriment of the subjective. The crucial decision takes place outside ourselves in the suffering and death of Christ, where our situation and destiny are irrevocably altered irrespective of personal faith. He can assert: "His [Christ's] life in all the narrowness of its limits is the theatre of the whole action of loss and salvation."[18] Yet Barth cannot be accused of ignoring the dimension of human response, since he is emphatic that what has already been achieved and enacted must be apprehended and acknowledged in the here and now.

The illustration has been given to me by a Barthian friend of a fugitive from justice who is granted unconditional pardon by a judge. The fugitive, of course, represents fallen mankind; and the judge, who takes the burden of the crime upon himself, is Jesus Christ. In this perspective the fugitive has already been set free, he is already emancipated, though he may not be aware of it. All he needs is to acknowledge this great fact and then to live as a free man. There is much biblical wisdom in this illustration, but what troubles me is that it overlooks the incontestable biblical truth that God's act of liberation in Jesus Christ does not take effect except in and through man's decision of faith. God's offer of pardon is not conditional upon man's worth or merit, but it is inseparable from the act of faith and repentance. The judge does not reckon man as righteous except through his faith (Rom. 4:5), and this means that the fugitive remains one until he appears before the judge and claims the writ of pardon as his own. His debts have been paid by the judge himself; yet the judge will not wipe the slate of the transgressor clean until he confesses his wrong-doing and promises not to run away from the law again. If he spurns the divine offer of forgiveness, the forgiveness is withdrawn, and he then stands under God's wrath to an even greater degree (cf. Matt.

22:1-10; Heb. 10:26-29).[19] The cause of God's mission of mercy is not the faith of men, but it is realized in their lives only through their faith.

Christ's salvation, to be sure, is more than an offer or invitation (and Barth never tires of stressing this): it is an accomplished victory. But this victory is realized not only on the Cross of Calvary but also in the hearts of believers as they are empowered to respond by divine grace. Christ performs his work of salvation not only outside of us but also within us by his Spirit. The locus of his victory is twofold: the events of the crucifixion and resurrection and the response of the believer. His work outside of us is in one sense complete, since he suffered once for all for the sins of fallen man; but in another sense it needs to be fulfilled by taking root within man, and this entails repentance for sin and total commitment to the cause of the kingdom. Barth sometimes speaks of salvation finding its goal in the obedience of faith, but for him man continues to stand under the verdict of salvation even apart from faith and even in opposition to faith. In this view Christ's confession of sin on behalf of man is sufficient to ensure man's liberation and redemption.

Another pertinent illustration is a man in one of the upper floors of a burning apartment building. A net has been provided, and he can now jump to safety. If he does not take this leap of faith he is doomed. On the other hand if he jumps it cannot be said that he saves himself, since he has been convinced by the Fireman in charge (Jesus Christ) that such an act is necessary and also perfectly safe, and it is the latter who has provided the net. From our perspective this illustration accurately depicts the situation of fallen man as he is confronted by the grace of God (cf. II Pet. 3:11-13; Heb. 11:13-16; Rev. 21:1, 2).

In the Barthian view the fire has been successfully put out, though smoldering embers as well as a certain amount of smoke and soot remain. This fact, however, is not known by the man in the upper story, who is under the illusion that the fire continues and that he is in mortal danger. He needs to be told that the danger has passed, that he can remain in the apartment building, which has now been reclaimed. Of course he needs to be delivered from his present agony, but what is significant is that his agony has no basis in reality.

Berkouwer cites another illustration that perhaps does more justice to the corporate nature of salvation as Barth understands this: the enemy city has been captured and the government has capitulated, but the news of this event has not yet reached all parts of the city.[20] In our view the powers of darkness have been decisively defeated, but they will not relinquish their *de facto* control of the city, even though in principle their kingdom has been taken from them.[21]

To Barth's credit he assigns a prominent role to the Christian life, not as a way of working out our salvation but as a proclamation and demonstration of the salvation Christ has wrought for all men. Barth is emphatic that grace not only saves but must also rule in the lives of men. Like Bonhoeffer he attacks cheap grace and stresses the need for costly discipleship. In his theology obedience is an integral element in faith. With the Reformers he insists that the Christian life does not procure salvation, but it attests a salvation already given. For Luther and Calvin if one is justified he will invariably live the Christian life. For Barth one should try to live the Christian life to show that he is justified.

In addition to justification Barth speaks much of sanctification. Yet sanctification is not a divine process within man by which man is transfigured in the image of Christ; rather it is a divine act by which all men have been changed in Jesus Christ. Nevertheless this divine act has concrete effects in the lives of men through the Holy Spirit. Barth is even willing to describe sanctification as a "real change" by which a new form of existence comes into being, "in which man becomes the true covenant-partner of God." [22] It is incumbent upon those who believe to reflect and manifest the objective work of sanctification in their lives. Just as we are justified by our faith so we are sanctified by our love. If Barth does not envision any kind of deification or entire sanctification for the Christian, he does acknowledge the need for the life of the Christian to become a concrete sign and witness of the perfect sanctification in Jesus Christ. He by no means denies the subjective dimension of sanctification, but his stress is on its objective basis in the personal history of Jesus Christ (cf. I Cor. 1:30).

Where Barth appears to move beyond the Reformation position in this area is in his view that the man in Christ can do works that are genuinely pleasing to God, works that are "really good," that manifest and give shape to our sanctification.[23] Because the man of faith has been baptized by the Holy Spirit into living communion with Christ, he is thereby enabled to follow his Master and to walk in his steps.[24] Man's new life is not as such infected by sin, but it is interrupted by sin, since man does not continually abide in Christ. Sin is ontologically impossible even for the unbeliever, who exists in hidden continuity with Christ, but especially so for the Christian, who is united with Christ in faith; yet sin nevertheless happens, and this is why we must constantly ask for forgiveness. While sin has been overcome totally and decisively in Jesus Christ, who includes all humankind within himself, this triumph is only imperfectly reflected in the lives of people, even the people of faith, who must still contend with sin. We need not sin, we now have the power to master sin, but we do sin time and again, and this accounts for the struggle as well as the victory in the Christian life. Good works do not win merit for us in the sight of God, they do not justify us before God, but they are works that God praises. They are good only because of their participation in the perfect work of God in Jesus Christ. They reflect and attest the grace of God that was revealed in Jesus Christ and that makes all good works possible. Barth acknowledges with the Reformers that our good works are not free from sin and ambiguity, but they are truly good because they have their foundation and goal in the grace of Jesus Christ; they "declare what God has done and accomplished—the goodness in which He has turned to man and given Himself for him."[25]

This praise of works is a welcome note particularly in view of the fact that good works have been denigrated by some overzealous sons of the Reformation (e.g., Amsdorf). Barth is on firm ground in his assertion that truly good works point beyond themselves to God's great work in Jesus Christ, that sanctification in its subjective dimension is an indispensable fruit and evidence of the objective work of reconciliation and redemption on Calvary.

While Barth sees the truth in Luther's formula *simul iustus et peccator,* he contends that this must not be taken to mean that the Christian is equally within the domain of sin and grace. Sin is now behind the Christian as he moves into a future that has been opened to him by divine grace. Though Barth concurs in the Reformation principle of the justification of the ungodly, he is just as insistent on the sanctification of the righteous. Yet he makes clear that man's own righteousness is but a broken reflection of the perfect righteousness of Jesus Christ, which alone is the basis of our pardon and redemption. Barth's restatement of an old theme may prove to be an ecumenical breakthrough insofar as he seeks to do justice to the Catholic concern for personal righteousness but within the context of *sola gratia.*

No less pertinent to the modern discussion in

soteriology and ethics is Barth's conception of freedom as the decisive hallmark of salvation. Here the Pauline strand in Barth's theology is conspicuous as elsewhere, for it was Paul who declared: "It is for freedom that Christ has set us free" (Gal. 5:1 New International Version). Barth contrasts true freedom, which is assured to man through the creation and incarnation, with false freedom, which is arbitrary self-assertiveness. What is often called "free will" comes under the rubric of false freedom, since it means a freedom to obey or disobey. It is likened to Hercules standing at the crossroads. True freedom is freedom to obey in the strength of faith, to live in accordance with the will of God. It is "never freedom to repudiate" one's "responsibility before God."[26] To be free means to be under the command of God and to allow this command to determine one's action. The liberated person chooses the possibility placed at his disposal by divine grace. True freedom is already ours by virtue of our creation and reconciliation through Christ. Yet we are not free practically until the knowledge of our freedom is brought home to us by the Holy Spirit. True freedom for God can only be used or unused; it cannot be misused. Disobedience consists in the neglect and disregard of true human freedom.

The question we have is whether man has not actually lost his true freedom through sin and consequently whether he needs to be given this freedom anew. For Barth it seems that true freedom is only obscured or hidden by sin, and man needs only to recognize it and exercise it. To be sure this recognition is dependent on the work of the Holy Spirit. Moreover, is not sin itself an abuse of man's freedom and not only a neglect? According to Barth freedom cannot be abused or misused, because its very meaning is to walk in conformity with the way of Christ. When we look to ourselves instead of to Christ we fall away from our freedom, but we never lose our freedom. In Barth's theology it seems that man is ontologically capable of responding to God's grace, but he is psychologically unwilling. He needs to be assured that his legs have not been broken by the fall, that he can walk if he would only look to Christ and trust in his Word. Yet, does not the new birth mean that man is given new legs, a new nature, a new heart so that he becomes both willing and able to obey the divine command, which was hitherto an impossibility for him?

While not sharing his expectation of a universal final salvation, I do affirm with Barth the doctrine of the universal atonement, namely, that Christ died for the whole world and not just for a select few. God's mercy is evenhanded, as well as his justice. Yet if the atonement is intended for all and is sufficient for all, it is efficacious only for some; and this is the truth in the Calvinist emphasis on the particular atonement. The fruits of the atonement do not extend to all, however, not because God has already arbitrarily consigned some to perdition but because man deliberately and irresponsibly rejects the message of the gospel. Here we see the irrational or surdlike character of sin, to which both Barth and Martin Kähler before him referred. The mystery, of course, is that even in man's rejection God is present, and man could not reject apart from God's sanction, just as he could not accept apart from the outpouring of God's grace. But it is entirely wrong to try to give this mystery a rational explanation by attributing man's damnation to a divine decree of damnation even before the creation.

Barth is quite right in affirming the universality of the Lordship and Saviorhood of Christ, but he goes too far when he suggests that all are in the body of Christ and the kingdom of Christ. He says that once we affirm, as we must, that Jesus Christ is "Head and Representative" of all men, then we cannot escape envisioning the body of Christ as "including and uniting all men."[27] In Barth's judgment one must also conclude on this basis that all history partakes in the history of salvation. He is not averse to affirming that "world history" is in reality "church history," though this truth is not generally known. He is here upholding a Christian universalism, not a syncretism that acknowledges the validity of the seminal insights in all world religions. Nor does he wish to imply that salvation has reached its goal in all people and in all religions. The covenant extends to all, but it is not yet concluded with all. The church is the visible fruit of the new humanity, which embraces all, but the significance of the gospel has not yet dawned upon all.

For Barth salvation is primarily and essentially an

objective occurrence in the past. What occurs in the present is man's response to this event by the power of the Holy Spirit. The world is already reconciled, though it looks forward to its final redemption. God's act of love in Christ changes the very being and destiny of man. In my view, on the contrary, the sacrifice of Christ changes God's attitude toward man or at least the way in which he deals with man, but man himself is not changed until he is convicted of sin by the Holy Spirit and brought to a saving faith in Jesus Christ. While Barth sees the need for man's personal participation in the salvation wrought for him in Christ, he is adamant that the essential change takes place wholly outside of man.

This brings us to Barth's distinction between reconciliation (Versöhnung) and redemption (Erlösung). He sees the former as primarily the work of Jesus Christ; the latter is peculiarly associated with the work of the Holy Spirit. While reconciliation is complete, redemption in its final state is yet to be unfolded. He speaks of the humanity that is "reconciled to God in Him [Christ]" but that is "not yet redeemed." [28] There are some New Testament passages where redemption is depicted as purely eschatological (Luke 21:28; Rom. 8:23; Eph. 1:14; 4:30), but for the most part it simply represents another side of the salvation purchased for us by Christ (cf. Gal. 3:13; 4:4, 5; Titus 2:14; I Cor. 1:30; Heb. 9:12). In Col. 1:13, 14, 20 Paul states that we are reconciled "by the blood of his cross," redeemed from the power of darkness and transferred into "the kingdom of his beloved Son." It should be recognized that Barth quite often also closely associates redemption and reconciliation, even describing redemption as "reconciliation without qualification."[29] Redemption will be the "full manifestation of the reconciliation of the world accomplished in Jesus Christ."[30] At the same time he can speak of "a fundamental difference" between reconciliation and redemption, since now we possess the blessedness of the eternal kingdom only in faith and hope.

Our view is that the world is not yet reconciled or redeemed, but the community of the faithful partakes now in both reconciliation and redemption. Paul definitely limits the scope of reconciliation when he says that Christ "has now reconciled [you] in his body of flesh by his death, . . . provided that you continue in the faith" (Col. 1:22, 23).

The atonement brings pardon (reconciliation) as well as deliverance from the power of sin (redemption). But can one have either reconciliation or redemption apart from the decision of faith? Can we even speak of the reality of the atonement apart from the surrender and obedience of faith? Assuredly in one sense we can, since salvation was procured in principle (*de jure*) for all men through the sacrificial death of Christ on the cross (II Cor. 5:14; Heb. 7:27). But though the gates of the prison have been opened we are not saved *de facto* until we rise and pass through these gates to freedom. "The grace of God," says the apostle, "has dawned upon the world with healing for all mankind" (Titus 2:11 NEB). With

Barth we affirm that this salvation is not simply a new possibility but a transforming reality that changes the face of history. Yet unless this revivifying grace penetrates the hardened hearts of people, unless they appropriate it in faith, it does not result in their actual deliverance from their sins. We acknowledge that the objective pole of the atonement is prior to the subjective, but it is fulfilled and completed in the subjective. For Barth, Jesus Christ signifies the subjective realization as well as the objective accomplishment of salvation, though he acknowledges that this reality must break into our lives in the "here and now." He is quite willing to include the salvation history of the covenant community within the subjective dimension of the atonement, but this history is already "enclosed and exemplified" in the history of Jesus Christ. There are times when it appears that the history of the church is simply the reverberation of the victory of Christ on the cross, whereas we see it as the battlefield on which this victory is carried forward to fulfillment.

Barth insists that we live in a reconciled and liberated world, but is this true? "The problem of humanity," Robert Paul observes, "is that it is unreconciled and unreconciling, and until this problem is met there can be no kingdom of God." [31] In Calvin's view: "Although conversion is not the ground of pardon, yet we know that none are reconciled to God but those who repent." [32] We can affirm that in Jesus Christ God is now reconciled to man, but can we say that man, all men, are already reconciled to God? Barth can say this because for him all mankind is included in the manhood of Jesus Christ.

He speaks much of the ministry of reconciliation, but this ministry is not the reconciling of man to God, which has already been accomplished in Christ, but the proclamation of this event to the world. It also entails the reconciling of man to his neighbor in the light of God's gracious act in Jesus Christ. Yet Paul declares: "We beseech you on behalf of Christ, be reconciled to God" (II Cor. 5:20). Barth refuses to interpret this as "an extension of the atonement in the form of something which man himself can decide."[33] Instead it is a request for an openness and obedience to God's gracious act of reconciliation in Christ, which has irrevocably changed the spiritual situation of man whether he believes or not.

In my view the victory of Christ over the powers of darkness benefits all, but it does not liberate all. It makes their liberation and reconciliation viable but not inevitable. Barth maintains that faith as the power of liberation comes to us as a new reality, not a new possibility. Insofar as faith is created within man by the Holy Spirit, Barth is in this sense right. Yet the reality of Christ's liberation is effectual in man's life only in faith. The work of Christ on the cross and personal faith are inseparably and organically related. No man can be in Christ but him who believes.

Berkouwer accuses Brunner of making the objective work of salvation in Jesus Christ and personal faith of equal significance.[34] In Berkouwer's view salvation and faith are correlative, but the former unquestionably takes precedence over the latter. Barth, as we have seen, goes still further and speaks of faith as only a correspondence to God's act of salvation in Christ, not as a correlative. "To *be* apprehended is enough," he says. "It requires no correlative on my side, and can have none."[35] In my view the objective work of salvation definitely has priority over faith in that it has cosmic significance affecting even the angelic creations and the world of nature. Yet for the individual Christian, faith is just as decisive, since apart from personal faith salvation is forfeited. Calvin contended that "as long as Christ remains outside of us, and we are separated from him, all that he has suffered and done for the salvation of the human race remains useless and of no value for us. Therefore, to share with us what he has received from the Father, he had to become ours and to dwell within us."[36]

Barth's apparent underplaying of the continual threat of evil and of the power of evil also invites criticism from those holding to an evangelical or biblical orientation. Conservative theologians in both Lutheran and Reformed circles have perceived a Platonic element in his theory of evil, though he does not treat it merely as a privation. Yet he speaks of it as "a shadow without real substance."[37] For Barth there is "no ontological godlessness": this means that evil is not in the created structure of existence as such even if it casts a pall over human existence.[38] "The possibility of existence which evil can have," he says, "is only that of the *impossible*, the reality of existence only that of the *unreal*, the autonomous power only that of *impotence*."[39] After the advent of Christ it assumes the "no longer dangerous form of a reminiscence and shadow of its former power" and becomes an "instrument of God's willing and doing." The principalities and powers of the world are "forced into the service and the glorification of Christ, and, through Him, of God."[40] They are now servants, though admittedly unwilling servants, of the kingdom of God and no longer adversaries. "Where God exercised His . . . wrath and judgment, He does so no more; but where he does so no more there is no enemy against whom to do so."[41] The devil continues to exist, but he is likened to a "wasp without its sting."[42] Markus Barth gives the illustration of barking dogs that are chained in order to underline the incapacity of the demonic powers to injure man.[43] In the Barthian view nothingness should be regarded as "finally destroyed." It would be inadmissible to suppose that "real deliverance and release from it were still an event of the future."[44]

I find this point of view difficult to square with that of the apostle Paul, who maintains that "we are not contending against flesh and blood, but against the principalities, against the powers, against the world rulers of this present darkness, against the

spiritual hosts of wickedness in the heavenly places"
(Eph. 6:12; cf. II Tim. 2:26). Nor can it be easily
harmonized with the admonition of I Peter: "Be
sober, be watchful. Your adversary the devil prowls
around like a roaring lion, seeking some one to
devour. Resist him, firm in your faith, knowing that
the same experience of suffering is required of your
brotherhood throughout the world" (5:8, 9). Barth in
the later volumes of his *Dogmatics* returns to a more
realistic view of the continuing battle between light
and darkness,[45] but he still sees darkness as lacking
any positive power or creativity. The antithesis
between the good creation and the Nothingness has
not been removed, but its edge has been taken from
it.[46]

In fairness to Barth it should be said that he
recognizes that the demonic force of evil even in its
nullified and defeated state can still cause trouble for
the Christian. The devil cannot alter man's justification and sanctification, but he can beguile man into
denying and doubting the reality of Christ's salvation. He retains a semblance of power by his lies and
deceit. Barth indeed reminds us that the devil is the
father of lies (John 8:44).

On the question of the relation of church and state,
I have considerable difficulty with his view that the
state, as well as the church, belongs to the order of
redemption. In traditional Reformed and Lutheran
theology the state was said to be in the order of
preservation, and the church alone was seen in the
order of redemption. Yet Barth's emphasis on the

universal Lordship of Christ has moved him toward the vision of a Christocracy in which the powers and principalities of the world become servants and emissaries of Jesus Christ. The church, he says, constitutes the "inner circle" of the kingdom of Christ and the world or state the "wider circle." The state, like the church, must serve the person and work of Christ and "therefore the justification of the sinner," though it does this in a different way from the church. The church preaches the message of justification, and the state implements and enforces justice. The state too is in the christological sphere. Yet the state, unlike the church, is not aware of the fact that it belongs to Jesus Christ. Because the state as such knows nothing of love and forgiveness it must continue to bear the sword, and it does not wield it in vain. Nevertheless, through the leaven of its Christian citizens the state can reflect the truth and reality that are in the church, for the center of both church and state is Jesus Christ. Barth acknowledges the reality of "demonic states" that become a law unto themselves and do not acknowledge any transcendent norm of judgment, but this is a perversion of the state's true being and purpose. Barth sees a definite continuity between the worldly city and the heavenly city (polis) to which all creation is moving. In contrast to Augustine he envisions not two cities in dire conflict with each other, but one city that in proleptic form already embraces both church and state though its revelation and fulfillment lie in the future. In my judgment

Augustine is closer to the biblical picture of the city of man remaining an adversary to the city of God until the very end of time.

Barth in his earlier years was very much influenced by Kierkegaard, though he discarded Kierkegaard's existentialism when he embarked upon his *Church Dogmatics*. It can be shown, I believe, that as Barth's theology developed, the gulf between his position and Kierkegaard's grew steadily wider. In many respects Barth is much more biblical than Kierkegaard, especially in his more positive attitude toward the world, as reflected, for example, in his doctrine of marriage. At the same time Kierkegaard's fidelity to the faith of the Reformation is more evident, it seems to me, in the area of soteriology, though he sometimes appears to verge on Manichaeism. The chasm between these two Protestant luminaries is especially noticeable in this statement of Kierkegaard's:

There is a nonsensical doctrine today that Christ saves *the human race*. This is balderdash. I'll even say that if Christ had wanted this he could not have done it, for the race is in the category of perdition and salvation is outside the race. . . . Yet today we are almost ready to identify being Christian with being human.[47]

In Kierkegaard's view man must be brought to despair by being confronted with the harsh words of the Law before he will turn to the Gospel in faith and repentance. He must be exposed to the message of God's wrath and judgment before he is ready to hear the glad tidings of God's grace and mercy. He must be awakened to the extremity of his need and the burden of his guilt before he is ripe for faith. "Take away the alarmed conscience," this theologian says, "and you may close the Churches and turn them into dancing halls."[48] Barth, on the other hand, maintains that the Gospel precedes the Law, that one cannot really know his need and sin until he is exposed to God's great love revealed in Jesus Christ. The Gospel is good news, and the Law as the form of the Gospel is included in the glad tidings. My view is that the Law and Gospel belong together, that both together bring knowledge of sin and both together serve as a pattern for the Christian life.

My reservations concerning Barth's position are that preaching for conviction of sin tends to be relegated to the background, and the content of our message seems only to be the announcement of God's grace and judgment already effected on our behalf in Jesus Christ. Indeed, it is precisely in the practical area of proclamation that the points of conflict as well as the affinities between Barth's position and historical evangelicalism are most conspicuous.

In maintaining that God's invitation extends to all, that his love is available for all, that all are claimed by his grace, Barth wishes to safeguard the open situation of preaching and hearing. Yet does he not err in claiming that all are in the kingdom of God's love irrespective of their response? He contends that in the church's missionary outreach our hearers should be approached not as sinners but as virtual brothers.[49] But does not this undercut or deny the reality of being spiritually lost?

Barth sees the content of Christian preaching as the kerygma, the message of reconciliation and redemption. It is not so much teaching or reflection as proclamation. "Preaching does not reflect, reason, dispute, or academically instruct. It proclaims, summons, invites, and commands."[50] Yet in his mind the preacher should not preach for conviction of sin or appeal for conversion.[51] This is because man's conversion has already taken place in Jesus Christ, and only the Holy Spirit can awaken the listener to this great fact. The Spirit is presumably at work as the pastor preaches, but he works not so much in and through the words of the sermon as with, over, and against these words.[52] In our preaching we should seek not to create a miracle but to bear witness to the one great miracle, realizing that an awareness of it may perhaps dawn in the minds and hearts of some people. Barth graphically explains his position: "Even with the most powerful and heartfelt appeal which it may make to them, it cannot change men. But with its appeal it can set before them the act of the love of God in which He has already changed them."[53]

In the sermon we should call our hearers to a life of discipleship, but it is not our place to offer them salvation. The gospel that we bring does not invite men to enter into a new freedom but "announces the transformation of our creatureliness into freedom."[54]

He criticizes the emphasis in much current preaching that "has to do with salvation in the future, something the preacher can help give, instead of speaking of the perfect salvation already accomplished." [55] In a sermon to the prisoners in Basel he declares: "We are not told: you may be saved. . . . No, you *have been* saved, totally and for all times." [56]

In Barth's eyes the preacher of the gospel should remind his hearers of the inescapable fact of sin and the need for continual repentance, but he should not threaten them with the terrors of sin, death, and hell. "Certainly it is necessary to speak of human sin and error," he says, "but only in order to show that sin is annihilated and error destroyed." [57] There are real powers of darkness, but these powers have been effectively overcome in Jesus Christ. "He has already won the battle, our battle. All we have to do is to follow him, to be victorious with him." [58] For Barth the primary focus in preaching should be on the overwhelming power of grace and the futility and weakness of human wickedness in the face of it.

He has assuredly grasped one side of the truth of the gospel, but in so doing has he not obscured another side of this truth? His theological and homiletical approach cannot easily be reconciled with these words of John: "He who believes in him is not condemned; he who does not believe is condemned already, because he has not believed in the name of the only Son of God. . . . He who does not obey the Son shall not see life, but the wrath of God rests upon him" (3:18, 36; cf. 8:47). Barth's position

131

also appears to conflict with Paul's warning that the coming of the lawless one will deceive "those who are to perish, because they refused to love the truth and so be saved" (II Thess. 2:10; cf. 11, 12). Again it is well to reexamine in this connection Heb. 12:25: "See that you do not refuse him who is speaking. For if they did not escape when they refused him who warned them on earth, much less shall we escape if we reject him who warns from heaven" (cf. 2:3; Luke 9:26). Barth insists that the preacher is not an agent of salvation but only a witness or herald. Yet Paul declares: "I have become all things to all men, that I might by all means save some" (I Cor. 9:22; 1:21; cf. Jude 22, 23; I Tim. 4:16; James 5:20).

Barth's stress on the finished work of salvation is perhaps a needed corrective to the view rampant in American folk religion that salvation is primarily and essentially an experience of the power of God in the here and now. Such a notion robs the historical atonement of its significance and efficacy, since the work of Christ on the cross is reduced to a mere preparation for the real salvific event, which takes place in man's present religious experience. An unbiblical subjectivism is very much in evidence in current revivalism, liberal process theology, the human potential movement, and the pastoral psychology movement. It is my contention that biblical faith is neither objectivistic nor subjectivistic but paradoxical in that the divine Word and human subject must be seen together in paradoxical or dialectical tension. While Barth has been critical of a "naive objectivism" as well as a rampant subjectivism, he has not been quite as successful in maintaining the paradox of salvation as have both Luther and Kierkegaard,[59] and I might add Emil Brunner and Reinhold Niebuhr. Yet, whereas some of Barth's compatriots in the neo-orthodox movement, in their effort to safeguard human responsibility, often came close to compromising their belief in the sole sufficiency of divine grace for salvation, Barth has for the most part remained true to the Augustinian and Reformed principle of the sovereignty of grace.

Existentialist theology of the Bultmannian variety, with its pronounced subjectivistic orientation, can also be justly accused of failing to give proper recognition to the efficacious work of Christ on the cross. In the theology of Bultmann salvation is the realization of authentic existence, which is occasioned as we confront the death of Christ on the cross, but the latter does not in itself effect salvation. Christ makes salvation possible by the impact of his suffering and death upon men, but he does not himself accomplish salvation by dying on the cross and rising from the dead. For Bultmann the cross of Christ is not a metaphysical event that affects the whole cosmos but an existential event that changes the subjective human consciousness. The transcendent, kerygmatic elements of the cross of Christ are relegated to inwardness. If I had to choose between Bultmann and Barth there is no doubt that my choice would be the latter, since the objective, historical foundations of the faith are preserved in his theology. Barth, in contrast to Bultmann, seeks to do justice to the biblical and evangelical doctrine of predestination, the eternal decision of God to save mankind in Jesus Christ.

It is well to remember that salvation has three dimensions: past, present, and future. It is not only a past accomplishment but a present experience and a future hope. Its foundation and pivotal center are in the past; its concrete realization in the lives of men is in the present; its consummation and fulfillment will come in the future, in the absolute future beyond history. All three dimensions are present in Barth's theology, but it seems that salvation as a past accomplishment and finished work is given undue significance. The futuristic dimension of salvation would indubitably have been given more weight by Barth if he had been allowed to complete Volume V of his *Church Dogmatics*, which was to deal with the doctrine of redemption. He has declared that redemption is more than reconciliation, but he also describes it as the full manifestation of reconciliation. Much that is ambiguous in this area would very likely have been clarified.

Emil Brunner accuses Barth, and not without some justification, of a "fundamental alteration of the Christian message of salvation." Brunner sees Barth as teaching that "everything has already been decided beforehand"[60] with the result that the decision of faith is no longer "deadly serious." Berkouwer also protests against what he describes as "the apriori character of grace" in Barth's theology. Yet if we are to take predestination seriously, we cannot avoid the conclusion that our salvation has its source and foundation in the eternal counsel of God.

When Brunner's criticism is weighed against Barth's understanding of evangelism and missions, it has some merit. As can be inferred from our previous discussion, Barth sees the missionary task of the church not as the conversion of souls but as the announcement of the good news of God's grace, which already encompasses all humankind. As he phrases it: "In evangelisation the concern must be ... to disclose positively that ... their salvation is assured and present to them."[61] While agreeing with him that the evangelistic mandate must be centered on the announcement of the good news, we contend that this good news is that salvation is available to people, not assured to them, and therefore such preaching must aim for the conviction of sins and conversion.

One further reservation must be voiced concerning Barth's theology. The disjunction that he sees between faith and religion has some merit but tends to obscure the truth that faith does not arise except in and through religious experience. Such experience is not the source or ground of faith, but it is certainly its medium. He acknowledges that Jesus Christ is the answer to man's religious yearnings and gropings, but when he speaks of the awakening to faith as the "abolition" and "dissolution" of religion, this seems to connote only (or at least primarily) negation while the true picture is one of fulfillment in the midst of negation. He is right that all human religion is tainted by sin, and therefore divine revelation cannot but disrupt and overthrow human religion. At the same time this revelation transforms and remolds the forms as well as the content of natural religious experience. Barth acknowledges a true religion, which is justified and purified by divine revelation and whose object and goal is Jesus Christ. While joining with Barth in his admonition that true religion is not mysticism, I think it unfair to regard mysticism as "esoteric atheism," since many of the greatest saints in the Christian church were mystics. It is more proper to affirm that there are marked tensions between the tradition of Christian mysticism, which leans heavily on Neoplatonism, and biblical faith, which is oriented more about revelatory events in history than Eternity. In a day characterized by a resurgence of religiosity and neo-mysticism, so far removed from biblical faith, it is well to pay heed to Barth's warning that revelation is the judge of religious experience and not vice versa.

Because Barth is a theological giant who towers above most of his predecessors and all of his successors and because he is a man who loved the Scriptures and tried to allow his thinking to be determined by the Scriptures, it is well to end on a more positive note. Barth is absolutely right that we as Christians should look upon every person optimistically. No one should be given up as lost, since God "desires all men to be saved and to come to the knowledge of the truth" (I Tim. 2:4). Our optimism is founded not upon the innate capacity of man to come to salvation (this is the covert Pelagianism that Barth vehemently assails), but upon the sovereignty and invincibility of God's grace. Barth reminds us that all are under the sign of God's gracious predestination; all are claimed by his love and for his kingdom. Nor are those who have not yet come to faith in Jesus Christ necessarily eternally condemned. They still must be regarded as spiritually lost, since they have not yet been brought to a saving realization of what God has done for them in Christ. With Forsyth we do not foreclose the possibility of the restoration of at least some unbelievers beyond the curtain of death.[62] Yet God's love must woo and win them, and even in this context there is no salvation apart from Christ and apart from faith.

Nonetheless our optimism must be tempered by the realization that those who defy and deny the grace of God, those who refuse to respond to his outstretched arms of love, are headed for eternal perdition. Such persons stand under the wrath and judgment of God. This is the sin against the Holy Spirit, the "sin unto death" in the absolute sense, for it means rejecting divine forgiveness. Barth also says that such persons stand under the fearful threat of God's judgment, and yet he describes them as only the "apparently rejected." The crucial point of difference between Barth and historical evangelical theology is that for the latter hell is not simply a threat but an assured judgment that will be pronounced on men at the end of the age and by Jesus Christ himself (Matt. 25; II Thess. 1:5-10). This means not that God's love and grace are absent from his final judgment or even absent from hell itself but that persistent and incorrigible unbelief meets finally with disaster in the face of and even at the hands of God's love and grace. Hell would here be interpreted as an inner darkness rather than an ontological darkness that is completely devoid of light, and this notion is definitely to be found in Barth's theology. Indeed, it can be said that he has prepared the way for a viable doctrine of hell, though he has not followed through on this. In the Barthian scheme, the man who rejects his election cannot suffer the damnation that Christ suffered for him, but he must nevertheless still suffer the fruits of his folly, though it seems not for an interminable duration.

We must take care, as Barth aptly says, not to build fences around God's grace, but we must also not bind God's grace to the principle that it must invariably result in eternal life or salvation. While he sometimes gives the opposite impression, he would certainly concur. Indeed, he has shown that it is possible to affirm both the universality and sovereignty of grace without necessarily falling into either a theoretical universalism or Arminianism,[63] though a tacit universalism seems to characterize the underlying thrust of his theology. He has not always maintained the tension between the universal triumph of grace and the impossible but nonetheless incontrovertible rejection of grace by sinful man; yet, as he himself has said, if one must err, it is better to err on the side of grace.

The church today can learn from this perceptive and sometimes provoking theologian. We can appreciate his valiant attempt to make the Scriptures central again in the science of theology. His rediscovery of the dynamic character of revelation can be of incalculable value to the church so long as its propositional dimension is not denied.

I also share his conviction that theology must be thoroughly Christocentric (though not christomonistic) and that the incarnation and atonement of Christ have cosmic significance. He reminds us that Jesus Christ is Representative Man as well as Revealing God; with Paul he vigorously affirms that in the crucified Christ all have died (II Cor. 5:14). Yet he sometimes creates the impression that one's own personal death to self is an inevitable corollary of the universal death of mankind effected in the cross of Christ, and here I would take issue with him. The election of all to salvation in Jesus Christ does not necessarily assure the eventual redemption of each and every person claimed by Christ; this is in accord with one strand in Barth but in obvious tension with another.

On the whole I am sympathetic with his doctrine of predestination, though I would seek to correlate it with man's struggle toward faith and his perseverance in faith. Barth's position that divine predestination cannot be separated from, and indeed is revealed and fulfilled in, the vicarious suffering and love of Jesus Christ is far more biblical, in my estimation, than the more traditional Augustinian and Calvinist conception of double predestination, by which a sizable portion of mankind is excluded from the very possibility of salvation from all eternity. Barth makes a place for double predestination, but he sees God taking the decree of condemnation upon himself in the person of his Son. In contrast to Luther and Calvin he refuses to posit a secret or inscrutable will of God that stands at variance with his revealed will in Jesus Christ.[64]

Barth's invaluable contribution is also apparent in many other areas of theology. His emphasis on free grace provides an effective rebuttal to modern Pelagianism and synergism, and his stress on costly grace is a necessary antidote to an orthodoxism that separates grace and works. His view that all believers are called by God to testify to their faith before the world in words and deeds is solidly rooted in both the Bible and the catholic tradition. His admonitions against confusing theology with either the philosophy or psychology of religion must be taken seriously by all who love the faith once delivered to the saints. His vigorous defense of the doctrine of the Trinity is to be applauded in a time when unitarianism is making unprecedented headway in the academic theological establishment. His reservations concerning ecumenism, that truth must not be sacrificed at the altar of church unity, merit careful consideration. Finally his keen awareness of the social dimension of sin, especially his warnings that genocidal weapons are a spiritual peril, a veritable abomination in the sight of God, must be taken to heart by those who fear God and honor his commandments.

Yet in our appraisal of Barth we must not accept him uncritically. He wishes his own work to be judged by the criterion of Scripture, and this I have tried to do, not by an exhaustive appeal to the text of Scripture (though there is a place for this) but by examining his insights in the light of the whole message of Scripture.

Barth seeks to be an evangelical theologian, and this means one who in his theologizing is "informed by the gospel of Jesus Christ as heard in Holy Scripture."[65] Yet he has not always succeeded in holding in balance the various emphases and strands in biblical faith. He is to be appreciated for his earnest concern to be biblical and evangelical. His valid insights should be appropriated; his insights that seem to conflict with the clear witness of Scripture need to be weighed and sifted. Barth wished not to found a school of Barthian theology but to be read with discrimination, especially in the light of Scripture. He cannot be considered a sure and safe guide in the theological quest when taken only by himself; yet when united with the faith of the Protestant Reformation and when purified and corrected in the light of the Bible and the church tradition, his contribution has inestimable value for the church universal.

The church will be forever indebted to Barth for his cogent reminder that Jesus is indeed Victor; that through his sacrificial life, death, and resurrection the powers of darkness have been vanquished; that sin, death, and hell have been overcome. We also need to affirm with him the incomparable reality of the outpouring of the Holy Spirit, for it is through the work of the Spirit of Jesus Christ that people are liberated in fact, just as they have been liberated at Calvary in principle (though as we have seen Barth sometimes depicts the objective liberation as complete and effectual apart from its subjective apprehension and appropriation).

Jesus is Victor because Jesus is God himself in human form, and no earthly or demonic power can withstand and defy the living God of the Bible, who is absolutely sovereign, who is the power above all the powers. The church needs to recover this indefatigable, holy optimism that inspired Barth to give a monumental prophetic witness to the church and world of the twentieth century. Such an optimism will not deny the harsh reality of evil, and though Barth sometimes gives the impression of underplaying this reality he nevertheless acknowledges it as still very much present, albeit in a negative and insubstantial form. While not being wholly satisfied with the way in which Barth delineates the problem of evil, I fully concur with him that the doom of the forces of evil has been assured through the resounding victory of Jesus Christ. Once the impact of this event has dawned upon them, once their inward eyes have been opened to the transforming reality of the cross and resurrection, people everywhere can face the future with hope and courage.

NOTES

Foreword

1. See Cornelius Van Til, *The New Modernism: An Appraisal of the Theology of Barth and Brunner* (Philadelphia: Presbyterian & Reformed, 1946).
2. Karl Barth, *The Preaching of the Gospel*, trans. B. E. Hooke (Philadelphia: Westminster Press, 1963), p. 80.

I. The Challenge of Barth

1. He has declared: "When I should arrive in heaven, I would make inquiries first of all concerning Mozart, and then next for Augustine and Thomas, then for Luther, Calvin, and Schleiermacher." Quoted in *Der Spiegel*, December 23, 1959, p. 81.
2. According to Barth the "theologians of the 19th century proceeded fundamentally along the lines of the 18th century Christian Enlightenment," though in contrast to the Enlightenment they focused their attention upon "man's supposedly innate and essential capacity to 'sense and taste the infinite.'" In Karl Barth, *The Humanity of God*, trans. Thomas Wieser and John Newton Thomas (Richmond: John Knox Press, 1960), p. 21.
3. Barth was often very strident in his criticisms of Pietism, but at the same time he was appreciative of the contributions of some of its leading figures, particularly Zinzendorf, Kierkegaard, and the Blumhardts. The earlier Pietism associated

with Spener and Francke had only a minimal influence upon him. Barth was compelled to break with Pietism because of its subjectivistic bent.

4. Barth in his earlier years wished to stand in that line of theological descent that includes Paul, Jeremiah, Luther, Calvin, and Kierkegaard. In his judgment Schleiermacher and Melanchthon belong to another ancestral line. See his *Word of God and the Word of Man*, trans. Douglas Horton (New York: Harper, 1957), pp. 196, 197.

5. In his later years Barth saw Jesus Christ himself as the only sacrament, the only bona fide means of grace, though he continued to make a place for Baptism and the Lord's Supper but as dedicatory rites, not as sacraments. He also abandoned the traditional Reformed doctrine of infant baptism in favor of believer's baptism.

6. Barth can even say: "Faith is not mine but God's." In his *Epistle to the Philippians* (Richmond: John Knox Press, 1962), p. 47.

7. Karl Barth, *Church Dogmatics*, I, 1 (Edinburgh: T. & T. Clark, 1949), p. 524.

8. Thomas F. Torrance, *Karl Barth: An Introduction to His Early Theology, 1910-1931* (London: SCM Press, 1962), p. 88.

9. The term "dialectic" was used by Barth and Brunner not in the Hegelian sense of a thesis and antithesis united in a higher synthesis but in the Kierkegaardian sense of an absolute paradox where contradictory ideas are held together in dialectical tension.

II. Barth's Continuing Relevance

1. Barth's impact is especially noticeable on Moltmann, Pannenberg, James Cone, Arnold Come, William Hordern, Frederick Herzog, and to a lesser degree Harvey Cox, Joseph Fletcher, and Paul van Buren. Bonhoeffer, too, even in his phase as a secular theologian, showed the unmistakable imprint of Barth. Barth's dichotomy between faith and religion prepared the way for Bonhoeffer's "religionless Christianity."

2. I do not go along with Friedrich-Wilhelm Marquardt, who argues that Barth's theology signified an effort to find a theological basis for revolutionary social involvement. See his *Theologie und Sozialismus* (Munich: Chr. Kaiser Verlag, 1972). For a report on this controversy see Markus Barth, "Current Discussion on the Political Character of Karl Barth's Theology" in *Footnotes to a Theology: the Karl Barth Colloquium of 1972*, ed. H. Martin Rumscheidt (Waterloo, Ontario: CSR Office, Wilfrid Laurier University, 1974), pp. 77-94. Also see George Hunsinger, ed., *Karl Barth and Radical Politics* (Philadelphia: Westminster Press, 1976). In this book Joseph Bettis says that Barth's "utopian vision and revolutionary method qualify him as a major force in the struggle for socialist humanism" (p. 171). For a cogent criticism of Marquardt's thesis see H. Hartwell's review article in *Scottish Journal of Theology*, Vol. 28, No. 1 (1975), pp. 63-72.

3. Barth, *The Word of God and the Word of Man*, p. 143. He also declared: "The revolutionary Titan is far more godless, far more dangerous, than his reactionary counterpart—because he is so much nearer to the truth. To us, at least, the reactionary presents little danger; with his Red brother it is far otherwise. With this danger we are vitally concerned." Karl Barth, *The Epistle to the Romans*, trans. from 6th ed. by Edwyn Hoskyns (London: Oxford University Press, 1933), p. 478.

4. See Karl Barth, "Poverty" in his *Against the Stream*, ed. Ronald Gregor Smith (London: SCM Press, 1954), pp. 241-46.

5. For Barth's role in the Confessing Church and the significance of the Barmen Confession see Arthur C. Cochrane, *The Church's Confession Under Hitler* (Philadelphia: Westminster Press, 1962).

6. See especially Hans Küng, *Justification: The Doctrine of Karl Barth and a Catholic Reflection* (New York: Thomas Nelson & Sons, 1964) in which the author maintains that Barth's position on justification and sanctification is in surprising accord with the historical witness of the Catholic church. Küng has lately veered toward the left in his theological stance. For a trenchant discussion of several Catholic critics of Barth, including Bouillard, Küng, and von Balthasar see

Grover Foley, "The Catholic Critics of Karl Barth" in *Scottish Journal of Theology* June, 1961, pp. 136-55.

7. G. C. Berkouwer, *The Triumph of Grace in the Theology of Karl Barth* (Grand Rapids: Eerdmans, 1956).

8. For a forthright commendation of Barth's theology by a socially concerned "young Evangelical" see Donald Dayton, "An American Revival of Karl Barth?" in *The Reformed Journal*, October, 1974, pp. 17-20; November 1974, pp. 24-26.

9. Although Barth held that the Christian should look forward to the dawning of social righteousness on earth, he cannot in the strict sense be regarded as a utopian, since for him the consummated kingdom of righteousness transcends man's highest social expectations and is a sheer gift of God, not the pinnacle of human achievement. Moreover, it transforms and does not simply perfect human history. Barth's position is a corrective to both a visionary utopianism and a socially enervating cynicism (often parading as "realism") that virtually consigns the world to the powers of darkness.

10. It is well to note that in Barth's *Protestant Theology in the Nineteenth Century*, trans. Brian Cozens and John Bowden (Valley Forge, Pa.: Judson Press, 1973), there is scarcely any mention of theologians in Britain and America.

III. The Objectivistic Slant

1. See Barth, *Church Dogmatics*, II, 2 (Edinburgh: T. & T. Clark, 1957), pp. 165, 166; III, 2 (T. & T. Clark, 1960), p. 144. Here can be seen Barth's supralapsarianism in which the eternal decision of grace precedes the fall. In infralapsarianism God's decision to show mercy follows the fall and is conditioned by it. Although Calvin was a supralapsarian, many in the Reformed church as well as Lutherans and Arminians recoiled from this doctrine, which, in its original form, seems to make God and not man responsible for eternal damnation.

2. Election or predestination could also be mentioned here, though Barth sees election not only as antecedent to creation but also as inseparable from reconciliation and redemption.

We might add that creation itself is regarded as an act of divine election and justification.

3. Barth, *Church Dogmatics*, III, 1 (Edinburgh: T. & T. Clark, 1958), p. 119.
4. *Ibid.*, II, 1 (Edinburgh: T. & T. Clark, 1957), p. 158.
5. *Ibid.*, IV, 3 a (Edinburgh: T. & T. Clark, 1961), p. 269.
6. *Ibid.*, IV, 1 (Edinburgh: T. & T. Clark, 1956), pp. 229, 230.
7. *Ibid.*, IV, 4 (Edinburgh: T. & T. Clark, 1969), p. 17.
8. *Ibid.*, IV, 2 (Edinburgh: T. & T. Clark, 1958), p. 314.
9. *Ibid.*, p. 290.
10. Note that for Barth reconciliation is already effected in the incarnation of Christ, though it comes to fulfillment in his atonement. Barth here bridges the traditional cleavage between Eastern Orthodox and Protestant thought on this subject. The historical Protestant stress, unlike that of early Catholic and Orthodox mysticism, has been on the cross over the incarnation.
11. Barth, *Church Dogmatics*, IV, 3 b (Edinburgh: T. & T. Clark, 1962), p. 716.
12. *Ibid.*, IV, 2, p. 582.
13. *Ibid.*, IV, 4, p. 22.
14. *Ibid.*, IV, 2, p. 291.
15. *Ibid.*, IV, 3 b, p. 500.
16. Note that Barth makes use of two terms for conversion: *Umkehr* and *Bekehrung*. The latter, which is used in Pietistic circles, refers almost exclusively to the personal experience of conversion, the interior awakening to faith. His principal term is *Umkehr* (and also *Umkehren*), which denotes both the vicarious turning of the world and man objectively accomplished in Christ and the turning worked out in man's life in the commitment of faith and baptism. *Bekehrung* is definitely subordinated to *Umkehr* in his theology.
17. Barth, *Church Dogmatics*, IV, 2, p. 560.
18. *Ibid.*, p. 566.
19. *Ibid.*, IV, 4, p. 39.
20. *Ibid.*, IV, 3 a, p. 247. Cf. his earlier statement: "Christ is the occasion by which men are enabled to apprehend themselves as existentially free." In his *Epistle to the Romans*, 6th ed., p. 285.
21. Barth, *Church Dogmatics*, IV, 3 a, p. 247.
22. *Ibid.*, III, 4 (Edinburgh: T. & T. Clark, 1961), pp. 577, 578.

23. *Ibid.*, IV, 1, p. 743.
24. *Ibid.*, II, 2, p. 422. It should be noted that Barth generally speaks of all human beings included in the election of Christ, though he sees this not as an *a priori* principle but as an ineluctable implication of the biblical witness. Universal election cannot be a metaphysical presupposition or rational conclusion, but it can be an affirmation of faith and hope.
25. For Barth's discussion of the *ordo salutis* see his *Church Dogmatics* IV, 2, pp. 502, 503, 507-511.
26. Arthur Cochrane prefers the term "Nihil" to "Nothingness" in the translation of *das Nichtige*, since this word as Barth uses it denotes not only that which is null and void but also that which is accursed and abominable. Also one should take care not to confuse it with "the Nothingness" of secular existentialist philosophy. Cochrane discusses the wide difference between the Barthian and the existentialist use of this term in his *Existentialists and God* (Philadelphia: Westminster Press, 1956).

    It could perhaps be said that in Barth's peculiar use of *das Nichtige* he married Plato's chaos, Heidegger's *Nichts*, and the German word *vernichten*, which includes the connotations of destruction and nullification. For Barth the Nothingness is that which has already been superseded or abrogated.

    It is difficult to determine the exact linguistic origin of the term *das Nichtige*. It was frequently employed by the German Romantics, but Barth's use of it can be adequately understood only in the context of his own theology. His conception of it certainly differs radically from that of Hegel, who envisioned it as historical reality in its fallen condition.

    Interestingly enough, Robert Jensen translates *das Nichtige* as "Nihility" in his *Alpha and Omega: A Study in the Theology of Karl Barth* (New York: Thomas Nelson & Sons, 1963).
27. Barth, *Church Dogmatics*, IV, 3 b, p. 697.
28. *Ibid.*, II, 2, p. 172.
29. Helmut Gollwitzer, ed., *Karl Barth Church Dogmatics: A Selection* (Torchbooks; New York: Harper, 1961), p. 145.
30. Barth, *Church Dogmatics*, III, 3 (Edinburgh: T. & T. Clark, 1961), p. 310. In this sense it is a discreative rather than a creative force.

31. *Ibid.*, IV, 3 a, pp. 260, 261.
32. Tillich affirms the reality of the demonic but not the reality of a personal devil. The latter is symbolic for the transpersonal form-creating and form-destroying force that creates a cleavage between existence and the depth of being. This demonic force or power becomes particularly virulent when embedded in social institutions.
33. Barth avers: "It [the chaos] is not an adversary to God, but only the shadow of His work which both arises and is at once dispelled by His wrath. But to the creature it is an adversary for which the creature as such is no match. To God it is no problem. But it is the radical problem which faces the creature." *Church Dogmatics* III, 3, p. 77. For Barth, God in himself stands above the antithesis of the creation and the abysmal darkness, but in Jesus Christ his Son, he enters into this antithesis and overcomes it. Barth can even say that the original antithesis is not between light and darkness but between God and darkness (*ibid.*, III, 1, p. 120), but the meaning here is God in Christ, not God in himself. Cf. *ibid.*, II, 2, pp. 163, 166. It should also be noted that salvation is primarily from the chaos and only secondarily from sin, which is man's succumbing to the abysmal darkness.
34. Note that Barth refers to the "chaos-reality" as the "rejected, uncreated world." *Church Dogmatics*, III, 1, p. 133; cf. p. 124. Since it is contingent on God's act of creation, however, it can be said to be "created" in an indirect sense (p. 117).
35. *Ibid.*, III, 2, p. 616.

IV. Reinterpreting the Atonement

1. For a contemporary discussion of the various views of the atonement see Gustaf Aulén, *Christus Victor* (New York: Macmillan, 1969); and Malcolm Furness, *Vital Doctrines of the Faith* (Grand Rapids: Eerdmans, 1973), pp. 55 ff. Both these authors draw a sharp distinction between the juridical or satisfactionist theory associated with Anselm and Aquinas and the classic or dramatic theory associated with Irenaeus

and other church fathers, as well as Luther. Aulén generally refers to the former position as the "Latin theory." See also J. N. D. Anderson, *Christianity: the Witness of History* (London: Tyndale Press, 1969), pp. 66 ff., who convincingly shows how the classic and juridical views can be reconciled. Also see Paul Althaus, *The Theology of Martin Luther*, 2nd ed. (Philadelphia: Fortress Press, 1970), who argues that Luther combines the Latin and classical concepts but with the former predominating (pp. 218-23).

2. Barth, *Church Dogmatics*, IV, 1, p. 766. For the role of Jesus Christ as victorious king see *ibid.*, IV, 3 a, pp. 165 ff.

3. *Ibid.*, IV, 1, p. 82.

4. Barth declares: "God does not need reconciliation with men, but men need reconciliation with Him." *Ibid.*, IV, 1, p. 74. Here can be seen a possible conflict with Luther and also Calvin, both of whom depicted God as both the Reconciler and the Reconciled. Yet the note that God is also in a sense reconciled in that his righteousness is satisfied is not absent in Barth. At the same time it cannot be denied that the main movement of reconciliation in Barth's theology is manward, the overcoming of man's enmity to God.

5. *Ibid.*, II, 1, p. 563.

6. *Ibid.*, p. 152.

7. *Ibid.*, p. 403.

8. *Ibid.*, p. 152.

9. Karl Barth, *A Shorter Commentary on Romans* (London: SCM Press, 1959), p. 70.

10. Barth, *Church Dogmatics*, IV, 1, pp. 486, 487.

11. See John Dillenberger's *God Hidden and Revealed* (Philadelphia: Muhlenberg Press, 1953), which includes a poignant discussion of the relation between God's love and wrath in Luther, Brunner, and Barth. See pp. 63 ff., 104 ff., 129 ff., 157 ff., 164.

12. Barth, *Church Dogmatics*, II, 1, p. 398.

13. *Ibid.*, II, 2, p. 124. Cf.: "Jesus Christ, in His solidarity with 'human nature which has sinned, could pay the penalty of sin' . . . and . . . in the power of His divinity, could 'bear the burden of the wrath of God in His humanity.'" *Ibid.*, II, 1, p. 400.

14. Barth writes that grace "radically excludes" the law of sin and death and deprives it "of its power." *Ibid.*, II, 2, p. 591. The

"rule and the validity and operation of that Law ceases." P. 592.

15. *Ibid.*, II, 1, p. 383.
16. *Ibid.*, p. 400.
17. Barth says that God's forgiveness "does not speak of a new purpose or disposition or attitude on the part of God. And least of all does it speak of any mitigation of the severity with which sinful man is rejected by God. Rather it speaks of the fulfillment of that rejection." *Ibid.*, IV, 1, p. 94.
18. It is interesting to note that Barth criticizes the kenosis doctrine not only on the grounds that it makes the incarnation problematical but also because it does not take into consideration that it is precisely in the humiliation of Christ that his deity is manifest.
19. Barth breaks with the traditional Reformed position in his contention that the two states of humiliation and exaltation do not follow each other in time but instead stand alongside each other. In holding that the humiliation is effected in the divine nature of Christ and the exaltation in the human nature, he possibly makes himself vulnerable to the charge of Nestorianism, since it seems that the two natures are no longer organically related, though this is definitely not his intention.
20. Colin Brown points out in criticism that in the New Testament, Jesus Christ is the universal criterion of judgment, not the universal object of judgment. He says that "the New Testament speaks of a judgment over and above that which Christ received in His own person. This is not just the awful scrutiny of the lives of believers. It is the judgment of all who are not in Christ and who have rejected God." (In his *Karl Barth and the Christian Message* [London: Tyndale Press, 1967], p. 134). Is not Barth correct, however, in saying that Christ has been judged in the place of all men? Yet we would add that a second and final judgment will follow on the basis of our response to Christ.
21. Barth, *Church Dogmatics*, IV, 1, p. 283.
22. Berkouwer remarks that one cannot escape the impression that "substitution" "has a wholly different meaning for him than it has in the confession of the Church." In his *Triumph of Grace in the Theology of Karl Barth*, p. 317.
23. G. W. Bromiley contends that "substitution" is an accurate

though not perfect translation of Barth's *Stellvertretung*. It can also be (and sometimes is) translated as "representation" and "substitutionary representation," though the former especially is not adequate in conveying Barth's meaning of Christ displacing us on the cross. In a personal letter to this author dated October 23, 1974.

24. In Barth's words: "Jesus Christ is not what He is—very God, very man, very God-man—in order as such to mean and do and accomplish something else which is atonement. But His being as God and man and God-man consists in the completed act of the reconciliation of man with God." *Church Dogmatics*, IV, 1, pp. 126-27. Our view is that the atoning work of Christ is initiated but not completed in the incarnation, and Barth too sometimes speaks in this way. Barth's actualistic understanding of the incarnation, as something that continually recurs, tends to blur the distinction between the person and work of Christ.

25. Barth, *The Epistle to the Romans*, trans. from 6th ed., p. 160.

26. Kant's distinction between the noumenal and phenomenal is definitely reflected in Barth's remark that he wishes "to see through and beyond history into the spirit of the Bible, which is the Eternal Spirit." *Ibid.*, p. 1. This statement also reflects the Kierkegaardian distinction between time and eternity, which, like the Kantian one, is not without some biblical foundation.

27. While he stresses the note of satisfaction, this is a moral satisfaction signifying the triumph of vicarious love, not the placating of the justice of God.

28. P. T. Forsyth, *The Work of Christ* (London: Independent Press, 1948), p. 222.

29. *Ibid.*, p. 182.

30. P. T. Forsyth, *The Cruciality of the Cross* (London: Independent Press, 1948), p. 99.

31. P. T. Forsyth, *The Christian Ethic of War* (London: Longmans, Green, 1916), p. 99.

32. Forsyth, *The Work of Christ*, p. 147.

33. J. McLeod Campbell, *The Nature of the Atonement* (New York: Macmillan, 1895), pp. 101, 117.

34. R. Swanton, "Scottish Theology and Karl Barth" in *The Reformed Theological Review*, January-April, 1974, (pp. 17-25), pp. 20-22.

35. Barth, *Church Dogmatics*, IV, 1, p. 172. Cf. *ibid.*, II, 2, p. 739.
36. Barth writes: "This one Righteous can be righteous in our place, can be obedient for our sake, only because He acknowledges our sin, and drinks to the bitter dregs the cup of temporal and eternal destruction which must follow our transgression." *Ibid.*, II, 2, p. 749. Cf. *ibid.*, II, 1, p. 398; *ibid.*, IV, 3 a, p. 442.
37. Forsyth, *The Work of Christ*, pp. 225, 226. Forsyth also prefers to speak of "solidary reparation" in describing the work of Christ (p. 164).
38. Barth insists that God in himself is impassible and unchangeable but in his condescension to the world, in his self-determination in Jesus Christ, he makes himself vulnerable to pain and suffering. See *Church Dogmatics*, II, 2, pp. 163 ff. Moltmann in his criticism of Barth at this point seems to uphold a God who is in and of himself passible and changeable, but such a God would no longer be sovereign in any absolute sense. See Jürgen Moltmann, *The Crucified God* (New York: Harper, 1974), pp. 79, 203, 249 ff., 280.
39. He declares: "Atonement is altogether the work of God and not of man." *Church Dogmatics*, IV, 1, p. 74.
40. Barth writes: "Even in the last extremity the Christian realises that he is spared this . . . affliction and passion, because it has been borne by the suffering of this One. . . . On the other hand, he certainly does suffer, and has to do so, as a witness of the suffering of this One." *Ibid.*, IV, 3 b, p. 637.
41. For Barth the reconciling and atoning work of Christ is complete but not the revealing work of the Spirit. It is also well to note that in his theology, revelation is a creative and regenerative as well as a cognitive event.

V. Universal Salvation?

1. See Berkouwer, *The Triumph of Grace in the Theology of Karl Barth.*
2. Barth, *Church Dogmatics* IV, 4, p. 21.
3. *Ibid.*, IV, 1, p. 503.
4. *Ibid.*, II, 2, p. 693.

5. *Ibid.*, p. 27.
6. See Joseph Bettis, "Is Karl Barth a Universalist?" in *Scottish Journal of Theology*, December, 1967, pp. 423-36.
7. *Church Dogmatics* II, 2, p. 423. Cf. "He [man] stands under the threat and danger of being damned. His condemnation hangs over him like a sword." *Ibid.*, IV, 3 a, p. 465.
8. *Ibid.*, IV, 3 a, p. 477.
9. *Ibid.*, p. 117.
10. *Ibid.*, p. 355.
11. *Ibid.*, pp. 355-56.
12. *Ibid.*, II, 2, p. 167.
13. *Ibid.*, IV, 1, p. 747.
14. *Ibid.*, p. 221.
15. In Barth's theology redemption (*Erlösung*) in its eschatological aspect is closely associated and virtually identical with consummation (*Vollendung*). Barth also occasionally uses *Erlösung* to denote the subjective salvation given by the Holy Spirit, but here too it has an eschatological significance, something we possess only in faith and hope. *Erlösung*, to be sure, is already in the past in anticipatory form in that it is foreshadowed in creation and reconciliation (*Versöhnung*), but more often Barth employs *Erretung* and *Befreiung* to denote the objective or past work of redemption and liberation. The primary meaning of *Erlösung* is eschatological.
16. Barth, *Church Dogmatics* II, 1, p. 438. Cf. *ibid.*, II, 2, p. 607. The word that is used in both of these passages in *Die Kirchliche Dogmatik* is *Erlösung*.
17. Barth, *Church Dogmatics*, I, 1, p. 530.
18. *Ibid.*, IV, 1, p. 247.
19. *Ibid.*, p. 213. Note that the words that Barth employs here are *Erretung* and *Heils*.
20. Karl Barth, *Christ and Adam*, trans. T. A. Smail (New York: Harper, 1956), p. 45.
21. Barth, *Church Dogmatics*, II, 2, p. 448.
22. See Robert Macafee Brown, *Frontiers for the Church Today* (New York: Oxford University Press, 1973), p. 42.
23. The early Barth could declare that "men can apprehend their unredeemed condition only because they stand already within the realm of redemption. . . . How could they bring themselves to sigh for the longed-for redemption, if they were

not already redeemed [erlöst] and already blessed?" In Barth, *The Epistle to the Romans*, 6th ed., p. 286.

24. Barth is often inclined to minimize the continuing power of the devil. He says that in the light of Jesus Christ the devil or the Nothingness no longer "counts as a cogent factor." Except "for our still blinded eyes" it no longer "implies a threat and possesses destructive power." *Church Dogmatics*, III, 3, p. 363. The traditional view is that the devil can still work sickness and death among men as well as devastate nature. He can also draw men into eternal perdition and hold them in spiritual captivity, though he has no power over the souls of Christians. Yet he can afflict even the people of God with bodily harm (cf. Job 2:7; II Cor. 12:7; Rev. 2:10).

25. Barth, *Church Dogmatics*, IV, 3 a, p. 316.

26. Barth writes: "Reconciliation is real reconciliation because it makes us men who wait and look and move towards the redemption which has already taken place for us and is ready for us." *Church Dogmatics*, II, 1, p. 510. The word that he uses for redemption in this context is *Erlösung*.

27. John Calvin, *Institutes of the Christian Religion*, ed. John McNeill, trans. Ford Lewis Battles (Philadelphia: Westminster Press, 1960), II, 16, 13, p. 520.

28. Barth, *Church Dogmatics*, II, 2, p. 183.

VI. Two Conflicting Orientations

1. It is commonly said that Barth began with a Platonic-Kantian stance (*Epistle to the Romans*, 1st ed.), moved through a Kierkegaardian phase (2nd ed.) and then finally embraced the Anselmian methodology. Joseph McLelland maintains that the Platonic-Kantian base remained a permanent element in Barth's theology. See his "Philosophy and Theology—a Family Affair" in Martin Rumscheidt, *Footnotes to a Theology: The Karl Barth Colloquium of 1972*, pp. 30-52. It should be noted, however, that as Barth progressed in his theology, he became more consciously theological and more circumspect in his use of philosophical terminology. He

certainly cannot be considered either a Kantian or a Kierkegaardian, despite the fact that he drew upon both these philosophies as well as others.

2. Both Kant and Schleiermacher signified the transition from the Age of the Enlightenment to the Age of Romanticism, with Schleiermacher standing more firmly within the latter movement. Romanticism differed from the Enlightenment in its emphasis on feeling over reason; yet it too made the happiness and fulfillment of man its major concern. In this sense it can be regarded as both a qualification and extension of the Enlightenment. Both movements comprise part of the wider movement of secular humanism, which had its beginnings in its modern form in the Renaissance. The term "Age of Reason" can be applied to both the seventeenth and eighteenth centuries. It can also denote the broad sweep of secular humanism encompassing the seventeenth, eighteenth, and early part of the nineteenth centuries.

3. Barth, *Against the Stream*, p. 60.

4. See Arthur C. Cochrane, "On the Anniversaries of Mozart, Kierkegaard and Barth" in *Scottish Journal of Theology*, (September, 1956), pp. 251-63. Cochrane points out in this illuminating article that Kierkegaard appreciates Mozart because he heard in him a no to the past, while Barth esteems Mozart because he heard a resounding yes to God's creation. Both Cochrane and Barth hail Mozart as one whose music has universal appeal and who thereby transcended the age in which he lived.

5. Note that Barth, like Mozart, recognizes a dark side to creation, but he does not identify this with the Nothingness that has been nullified and abrogated by God. He concurs with Mozart that creation in its totality is good and praises God.

6. Barth, *Church Dogmatics*, III, 3, p. 298. It is significant that Barth had a generally high regard for the music of the eighteenth century and viewed it as vastly superior to the music of other periods.

7. In contrast to the Enlightenment Barth does not incorporate sin and evil into the good creation of God. For Leibniz the shadowy side of human existence is not eliminated but assimilated and becomes a necessary aspect of the whole. For Barth evil is negated and transcended, and this is why God's glory is mirrored and his purposes are fulfilled in the world.

God's yes to the world includes a no to its sin and corruption, and the no is made to serve the yes. There is a predetermined harmony because of the triumph of good over evil, a triumph already effected at the creation and revealed and fulfilled in the incarnation. This means that the world is accepted and justified despite the pall that evil casts upon it. See *Church Dogmatics*, III, 1, pp. 385, 388 ff.

8. Karl Barth, *Theology and Church*, trans. Louise Pettibone Smith (New York: Harper, 1962), p. 343.

9. While Barth sees faith as rational, not irrational, anti-rational, or supra-rational, he depicts sin as irrational and anti-rational. On the rational character of faith see his *Dogmatics in Outline*, trans. G. T. Thomson (New York: Philosophical Library, 1949), p. 23. It should also be recognized that for Barth the object of faith is fully rational. Indeed, God is likened to "self-sufficient rationality" as over against the "superessential One" of Neo-Platonic mysticism which transcends rationality. For a discussion of the role of mystery in a faith whose object is fully rational see Thomas Torrance, *Karl Barth: An Introduction to his Early Theology 1910–1931*, p. 82.

10. Barth, *Church Dogmatics*, IV, 4, p. 28.

11. John D. Godsey, ed., *Karl Barth's Table Talk* (Edinburgh: Oliver & Boyd, 1963), p. 31.

12. For a penetrating analysis of Barth's concept of freedom see Ulrich Hedinger, *Der Freiheitsbegriff in der Kirchlichen Dogmatik Karl Barths* (Zurich: Zwingli Verlag, 1962).

13. While Kant recognized the existence of a malignant force within man which he termed "radical evil," he nonetheless insisted that there still remains hope for man because he possesses a good will. He envisioned within man a "seed of goodness" that "still remains in its entire purity, incapable of being extirpated or corrupted." In his *Religion Within the Limits of Reason Alone*, trans. Theodore M. Greene and Hoyt H. Hudson (New York: Harper, 1960), pp. 39-41.

14. Barth, *Church Dogmatics*, III, 3, p. 161.

15. Barth, *The Word of God and the Word of Man*, p. 52. In one sense Barth's remarks apply especially and peculiarly to Christians, since it is they who generally come to the Bible with questions. But in another sense his remarks are applicable to all people, since all are encompassed by an

original divine yes that the divine no to human sin cannot eradicate (cf. p. 54). For Barth, even the early Barth, all are insiders by virtue of the universal election and atonement of Jesus Christ. He says that "thinking in terms of the humanity of God, we cannot reckon in a serious way with *real* 'outsiders,' with a 'world come of age,' but only with a world which *regards* itself as of age. . . . Thus the so-called 'outsiders' are really only 'insiders' who have not yet understood and apprehended themselves as such." He goes on to point out that even the most convinced Christian will at times feel himself to be an outsider, though no one is ever a bona fide outsider, since all are claimed by Christ and included in Christ. In Barth, *The Humanity of God*, pp. 58, 59.

16. Barth, *Church Dogmatics*, IV, 3 a, p. 146.
17. Cf. Luther: "No matter which way you look at it, the devil is the prince of this world." *Luther's Works*, Vol. 37 (Philadelphia: Muhlenberg Press, 1961), p. 18.
18. Barth, *Church Dogmatics*, III, 3, p. 367 (italics mine).
19. Whereas Luther and other Reformers saw the devil as the dire enemy of God, his first and most powerful opponent who is able to challenge the kingdom of the blessed, they nevertheless regarded him as an unwitting tool of God's wrath. God rules through the devil by his left hand just as he rules through Jesus Christ by his right hand.
20. From the 2nd edition of his *Epistle to the Romans*. Quoted in Hans Urs von Balthasar, *The Theology of Karl Barth*, trans. John Drury (New York: Holt, Rinehart & Winston, 1971), p. 56.
21. Von Balthasar, *The Theology of Karl Barth*, p. 81.
22. For Thielicke's criticisms of Barth's monistic orientation see Helmut Thielicke, *Theological Ethics*, Vol. I, ed. William Lazareth (Philadelphia: Fortress Press, 1966), pp. 98ff.
23. Barth, *Church Dogmatics*, IV, 1, p. 492.
24. Barth, *The Humanity of God*, p. 60.
25. Barth, *Christ and Adam*, p. 89.
26. Martin Luther, *Luther's Works*, Vol. 45, ed. Walther Brandt (Philadelphia: Muhlenberg Press, 1962), p. 90.
27. Barth, *Protestant Theology in the Nineteenth Century*, p. 233.
28. Barth, *Theology and Church*, pp. 353, 354.
29. Barth can even say that all people are created in the image of Jesus Christ, since the world was created through him.

30. Barth, *Church Dogmatics*, III, 2, p. 150.
31. John Calvin, *Reply to Sadoleto* in Hans J. Hillerbrand, ed., *The Protestant Reformation* (New York: Walker & Co., 1968), p. 162. Barth too can speak of man's lostness. See his *Church Dogmatics* IV, 1, p. 221.
32. Barth, *Against the Stream*, p. 239.
33. Barth, *Church Dogmatics*, III, 4, pp. 385-97.
34. Karl Barth, *Evangelical Theology*, trans. Grover Foley (Anchor Books; Garden City, N.Y.: Doubleday, 1964), p. 9.
35. There must be "no relegating of our hopes to a Beyond" but we must commit ourselves "to the task of affirming him [God] in the world as it is and not in a false transcendent world of dream." *The Word of God and the Word of Man*, pp. 317, 299.
36. Arthur Cochrane recounts: "One of my earliest and lasting impressions of Karl Barth is that he was a remarkably unreligious man. He once said: 'I will not build a Christian home.'" In Arthur C. Cochrane, "The Karl Barth I Knew" in Rumscheidt, ed., *Footnotes to a Theology: The Karl Barth Colloquium of 1972* (pp. 142-48), p. 143. It should be noted, however, that though he did not parade his piety, Barth was nevertheless a man of faith and prayer as was conspicuously apparent in his preaching. He was opposed to religiosity, where religion becomes conscious of itself as a religion. For him true religion breaks out of a concern with interior spirituality into loving service of one's fellowman.
37. Barth, *Church Dogmatics*, III, 3, pp. 264-65; III, 4, pp. 87-88. Already in his *Epistle to the Romans* (6th ed.) he described prayer as "an ethical action," p. 458.
38. The Reformers also stressed the need for social service but subordinated this to the glory of God and the conversion of souls to the kingdom of Christ. Barth sees the service of our fellowman as glorifying God but not so much as a means to the building or extension of the kingdom. He is hostile to any kind of Christian imperialism or triumphalism.
39. This pattern of thinking is further developed by Arthur Cochrane in his *Eating and Drinking with Jesus: An Ethical and Biblical Inquiry* (Philadelphia: Westminster Press, 1974) where the lines between the Lord's Supper and the common meal are virtually erased. For Cochrane even atheists in their eating and drinking partake of the meaning of the Supper.
40. Cf. Calvin: "For there is no other way to enter into life unless

this mother [the Church] conceive us in her womb, give us birth, nourish us at her breast, and lastly, unless she keep us under her care and guidance until, putting off mortal flesh, we become like angels." *Institutes of the Christian Religion*, IV, 1, 4, p. 1016.

41. Barth, *Church Dogmatics*, IV, 3 a, p. 33.

42. He would have much difficulty in saying with Luther: "Therefore, we who are in the ministry of the Word have this comfort, that we have a heavenly and holy office; being legitimately called to this, we prevail over all the gates of hell." *Luther's Works*, Vol. 26 (St. Louis: Concordia Publishing House, 1963), p. 20. While all Christians share in the general ministry of the Word, Luther saw the call to the public ministry as issued through the church and therefore as coming from Christ himself.

43. Barth envisions not a spiritualized existence for man in a supernatural realm beyond this world (as in Aquinas and Calvin) but a new corporeal existence for man in a world transfigured by the reality of the supernatural God. He says that the goal of history is "the summation of the history of God in history" and our hope is "the corporeality of the resurrection and the new world." *The Word of God and the Word of Man*, pp. 322, 93. This is strikingly similar to Bonhoeffer's upholding of a "historical redemption" over the "myths of salvation" which offer men deliverance into a supernatural or transcendent realm. See his *Letters and Papers from Prison*, trans. Reginald Fuller, ed. Eberhard Bethge (New York: Macmillan, 1967), p. 205.

44. Barth, *Protestant Theology in the Nineteenth Century*, p. 134.

45. Bernard Meland and Henry Nelson Wieman, *American Philosophies of Religion* (New York: Willett, Clark & Co., 1936), pp. 84 ff.

46. Barth was highly critical of what he termed the "gnostic occultism" of Rudolf Steiner and Anthroposophy and argued that the presuppositions of liberal theology lead in this direction. See H. Martin Rumscheidt, *Revelation and Theology: An Analysis of the Barth-Harnack Correspondence of 1923* (London: Cambridge University Press, 1972), pp. 35, 129, 130. Clyde L. Manschreck interestingly shows that the Protestant Reformers—Calvin, Luther and Melanchthon—were amazingly open to the world of the occult: dreams,

visions, stars, demons, etc. See his "Occult Tradition in the Reformation" in *Spiritual Frontiers,* Autumn, 1974; Winter, 1975, pp. 101-14.

47. Barth, *The Word of God and the Word of Man,* p. 70.
48. While Barth holds with the Reformers that unbelief is the core of sin, he sees idolatrous religion as a more insidious manifestation of sin than theoretical atheism. He can even equate religion with "unbelief, superstition and idolatry," though he acknowledges the reality of a true religion in which man's religious yearnings and rites are cleansed and transformed by divine revelation.
49. Von Balthasar, *The Theology of Karl Barth,* p. 202.
50. It is well to note that while Marxism can legitimately be viewed as the late harvest of the Enlightenment, National Socialism signaled a return to the gods of ancient tribalism.
51. For Barth there is no direct identity between the Bible and revelation, but there is an indirect identity in that the Bible ever again becomes revelation when the Holy Spirit works upon the hearts and minds of believers disclosing its inner truth. The Bible *is* the Word of God insofar as Jesus Christ by his Spirit reveals himself and the truth of the gospel in and through the very worldly language of the biblical writers.

While stressing the event character of revelation in conjunction with the Bible in his *Church Dogmatics,* I, 1, Barth establishes an ever more intimate bond between Scripture and revelation in his *Church Dogmatics* I, 2 (Edinburgh: T. & T. Clark, 1956), though still refusing to posit a direct identity between them. He now not only affirms the "distinctiveness" of Scripture from revelation but also "its unity with it, in so far as revelation is the basis, object and content of this word" (p. 463). He also declares that "what is said in the biblical word of man is divine revelation" and that "God's revelation in the human word of Holy Scripture not only wants but can make itself said and heard" (p. 471). And again: "Scripture is Holy Scripture as the witness of divine revelation . . . in such a way that the revelation of God is manifest in its witness demanding and receiving obedience as the Word of God" (p. 495). For Barth the Scriptures not in and of themselves but illumined by the Spirit are divine revelation.

52. Bernard Ramm, *The Evangelical Heritage* (Waco, Texas: Word Books, 1973), p. 119.
53. Barth, *Church Dogmatics* II, 1, p. 351.
54. *Ibid.*, p. 359.
55. It can be shown that the anthropocentric theology of the nineteenth century, what Barth called "Neo-Protestantism," had its immediate roots in the humanistic philosophy of the Enlightenment. Barth's tirade against Neo-Protestantism is indirectly a critique of the Enlightenment. At the same time, in his criticisms of the nineteenth century Barth sometimes appears to return to a rationalistic posture endemic to the seventeenth and eighteenth centuries. He never upholds an autonomous reason but reason in the service of faith. Pannenberg in his stress on reason before faith is much closer in this respect to the Enlightenment.
56. Barth, *Church Dogmatics*, IV, 1, p. 487.
57. Barth even maintains that the *non posse peccare* (the impossibility of sinning) becomes a possibility for man in this life. He makes clear that "in our union with Christ it is true for us. We can sin only far away from Christ, but not in and with Him." *Karl Barth's Table Talk*, p. 69. Cf. *Church Dogmatics* III, 2, p. 197; *ibid.*, IV, 2, pp. 495, 733. In this connection cf. I John 3:9; 5:18.
58. Barth, *Theology and Church*, p. 344.
59. Barth, *Church Dogmatics*, IV, 3 a, p. 350.
60. *Ibid.*, IV, 3 b, p. 877. In this respect Barth shows his distance from Pietism and his affinities with rationalism.
61. Barth, *The Word of God and the Word of Man*, p. 58.
62. Despite Pannenberg's quite pronounced rationalistic thrust Robert Jensen cautiously suggests that "Pannenberg is Barth inside out: Barth with past and future reversed, and therefore with history as a whole replacing analogous eternity." In his *God after God: The God of the Future, Seen in the Work of Karl Barth* (Indianapolis: Bobbs-Merrill, 1962), p. 179.
63. See Karl Barth, *Anselm: Fides Quaerens Intellectum* (Richmond: John Knox Press, 1930).
64. For a penetrating discussion of the early debate between Barth and Brunner on the "point of contact" between the gospel and secular man and the later position of Barth on the question of communication and apologetics see James E.

Sellers, *The Outsider and the Word of God* (Nashville: Abingdon Press, 1961), pp. 35ff. For the original discussion see Emil Brunner and Karl Barth, *Natural Theology*, trans. Peter Fraenkel (London: Centenary Press, 1946).

65. Barth makes this astute comment: "Kant both has and demands an almost unconditional faith in reason. But the only kind of reason he considers worthy of his trust is the reason which has first of all come to be reasonable as regards itself." In his *Protestant Theology in the Nineteenth Century*, p. 271.

66. Peter Gay, *The Enlightenment: An Interpretation* (New York: Alfred A. Knopf, 1966), I, 141.

67. Barth affirmed the moral absolute of the divine commandment but denied the universal or absolute validity of moral values that in his mind are conditioned by culture and history. To elevate what is culturally conditioned to absolute status is a monument to human hubris.

68. The term *Urgeschichte* was borrowed by Barth from the religious skeptic Franz Overbeck who deplored "a Christianity subordinated to time." He saw the historicizing of Christianity as its great betrayal.

69. Johann Semler (d. 1791), professor in Halle, is a typical representative of the "Christian Enlightenment," as Barth understands this. In him Pietism and rationalism came together, with the latter becoming more dominant as he developed his position. Semler anticipated some of the concerns of neo-orthodoxy in his distinction between the Bible and revelation. He was even more a precursor of the later liberal theology in his preference for a free, private religion of an ethical character over dogmatic, formalistic Christianity. Toward the end of his life he dabbled in esoteric mysticism. For Barth's criticisms of Semler see his *Protestant Theology in the Nineteenth Century*, pp. 169-71.

70. Similarly he refers to true evangelical theology as "theoanthropology," since it is "concerned with God as the God of *man*, but just for this reason, also with man as *God's* man." Barth, *Evangelical Theology*, p. 9.

71. Barth, *Church Dogmatics*, IV, 2, p. 6.

72. To be sure, the call for religious toleration and freedom stemmed partly from a latitudinarianism that downgraded the reality of the supernatural and the particularity of the

biblical revelation. But it also had its source in Pietism with its emphasis on the church as a voluntary association of true believers. The groups that came out of the revivals pressed for a disestablished church where membership is a matter of personal decision, not a legal necessity. In addition the emphasis on experience over doctrine in the circles of Pietism contributed to a climate of religious toleration.

73. On the confrontation between Barth and Harnack see Rumscheidt, *Revelation and Theology: An Analysis of the Barth-Harnack Correspondence of 1923.* Harnack hailed the Enlightenment as that period which gave clarity and maturity to scientific theology. Barth's theological approach was quite unacceptable to Harnack and vice versa.

74. An interesting study could be made of the impact of Pietism on Barth, which was considerable. Barth in his earlier years generally regarded Pietism as one element in the Enlightenment, and perhaps it could even be argued that Barth was influenced to some degree by the Enlightenment through Pietism. Among those in the tradition of Pietism who made an indelible impression on Barth were Zinzendorf, Kierkegaard, and the two Blumhardts. The influence of J. A. Bengel, who Barth says reflected certain concerns of the "Christian Enlightenment," was also significant. One such study on this subject has appeared, though its concentration is on the relation between Barth and Zinzendorf. See Frederick Gärtner, *Karl Barth und Zinzendorf: die bleibende Bedeutung Zinzendorfs auf Grund der Beurteilung des Pietismus durch Karl Barth* (Munich: Chr. Kaiser Verlag, 1953). My contention is that the mainstream of Evangelical Pietism signified the fulfillment of the Reformation and was a counterforce to the secular trends of the Enlightenment. See Donald G. Bloesch, *The Evangelical Renaissance* (Grand Rapids: Eerdmans, 1973), pp. 101 ff.

75. For Barth the ideal philosophy is one that will stay clear of any metaphysical synthesis and restrict itself to judgments of an analytic and descriptive character. It will acknowledge the limitations of rational inquiry, and therefore its contribution will be tentative and penultimate. It will see itself as a limited and critical exercise in epistemology (à la Kant?). Theology can lend its support to this kind of philosophy, but unfortunately philosophy generally does not remain within

this narrow framework. See Joseph C. McLelland, "Philosophy and Theology—a Family Affair" in Rumscheidt, *Footnotes to a Theology: The Karl Barth Colloquium of 1972,* pp. 30-52.

VII. Barth in Retrospect

1. Barth uses the metaphors of a chess game and a clock to underline his belief that Christ's victory is already an accomplished fact: "The game is won, even though the player can still play a few further moves. Actually he is already mated. The clock has run down, even though the pendulum still swings a few times this way and that." *Dogmatics in Outline,* p. 123. He goes on to point out that the adversary still acts as if "the game were not decided, the battle not fought." This means that any opposition can now have only the force of a mirage.

2. He declares: "We have described the sanctification of man, his existence as that of one of those who are judged by God, as a fact which is already completed, which has been factually and objectively created." *Church Dogmatics* II, 2, p. 774. And again: "It [salvation] is not intrinsic to ourselves but extrinsic." *Ibid.,* p. 645.

3. *Ibid.,* IV, 3 a, p. 179.

4. Barth, *The Epistle to the Romans,* 6th ed., p. 285.

5. Barth, *Church Dogmatics,* IV, 1, p. 148.

6. *Ibid.,* IV, 3 a, p. 220.

7. Godsey, *Karl Barth's Table Talk,* p. 92.

8. *Ibid.,* p. 87.

9. Barth, *Church Dogmatics,* IV, 1, p. 749. Barth says that as a human act of acknowledgement faith has only a cognitive character, but it is nonetheless accompanied and undergirded by the energizing work of the Holy Spirit.

10. Helmut Gollwitzer, *The Existence of God as Confessed by Faith* (Philadelphia: Westminster Press, 1965), p. 139.

11. Arnold Come, *An Introduction to Barth's "Dogmatics" for Preachers* (Philadelphia: Westminster Press, 1963), p. 30.

Other dangers that Come sees in Barthianism are: the absorption of humanity in Christ, the relativizing of history, and the limitation of the church's mission to simply the announcement of the good news.

12. Martin Luther, *Luther: Lectures on Romans*, ed. and trans. Wilhelm Pauck (Philadelphia: Westminster Press, 1961), p. 155.

13. See Althaus, *The Theology of Martin Luther*, p. 213. Calvin, too, speaks of faith reconciling us by joining us to God. *Institutes*, III, 2, 30.

14. Jonathan Edwards, "An Humble Inquiry into the Qualifications for Full Communion in the Visible Church of Christ," in *Works of President Edwards*, ed. Sereno E. Dwight (New York: S. Converse, 1829–1830), IV, 321.

15. Note that this statement does not in and of itself rule out the possibility of final universal salvation. Nor does it necessarily support the older Calvinist version of limited atonement, which affirms that Christ died only for a select few and that the destiny of both believers and unbelievers has already been totally determined prior to, and it would seem quite apart from, their actual response. In my view the crisis of salvation is a paradox that transcends and defies any air-tight logical explication or conclusion. This means that we can never assert the reality of divine election apart from the corresponding reality of faith and vice versa. For a further discussion of this rationally insurmountable mystery see my book *The Christian Life and Salvation* (Grand Rapids: Eerdmans, 1967).

16. Godsey, *Karl Barth's Table Talk*, pp. 15, 87.

17. For a cogent defense of Barth against the charge of objectivism see Herbert Hartwell, *The Theology of Karl Barth* (Philadelphia: Westminster Press, 1964), Hartwell admits, however, that Barth does not succeed in clarifying the relation between the objective and subjective aspects of reconciliation (p. 187). For Come's criticisms of Barth's objectivism see his *Introduction to Barth's "Dogmatics" for Preachers*, pp. 158ff.

18. Barth, *Church Dogmatics*, IV, 1, p. 756.

19. Barth approaches this truth when he says that "the man who does not recognize and accept and obey this decision, who does not believe, cannot count on anything but the wrath of

God, and even now that the clear day has broken, can exist only in darkness and corruption." *Ibid.*, p. 393. Yet Barth would not say that God withdraws his pardon or abandons man to the darkness.

20. Berkouwer, *The Triumph of Grace in the Theology of Karl Barth*, p. 265. Berkouwer also refers to Brunner's illustration of men on a stormy sea who are fearful of shipwreck. Yet they are in no danger of drowning because in reality they are in shallow water, only they do not know it. Berkouwer comments that this is an accurate portrayal of how Barth understands the situation of man which has been objectively altered by Jesus Christ (pp. 264, 265). What is needed is a subjective correspondence to the new objective situation in which mankind finds itself.

None of the preceding illustrations do justice to the totality of the Barthian schema, since they do not take into consideration Barth's emphasis that we are buried and raised in Christ, but they do accurately portray the situation of man after the atoning event. No illustration can sufficiently portray a theology as complex as that of Barth, and this is why it is not advisable to give it more weight than it can bear.

21. Though Barth often says that our salvation has been achieved *de jure* and not *de facto*, it seems that the latter simply means the subjective acknowledgement of salvation. The fuller statement of his view is that we are saved in reality as well as in principle, but this reality or actuality needs to make contact with our personal subjectivity if we are to have assurance of this salvation.

22. Barth, *Church Dogmatics*, IV, 2, p. 525.

23. *Ibid.*, p. 596.

24. Barth describes Christian discipleship as a "'following in his footsteps,' . . . an imitating of God as beloved children, . . . a perfection corresponding to the perfection of our Father in heaven." *Church Dogmatics*, III, 4, p. 649. Barth does not hesitate to urge the *imitatio Christi* which in his mind means a correspondence to the attitude and action of Jesus. *Ibid.*, IV, 1, p. 634.

25. *Ibid.*, IV, 2, p. 590.

26. *Ibid.*, III, 2, p. 197. Barth might have difficulty in harmonizing this view with Deut. 30:15, 16: "See, I have set before you this day life and good, death and evil. If you obey the command-

ments of the Lord . . . the Lord your God will bless you in the land which you are entering to take possession of it."

27. Barth, *Church Dogmatics*, IV, 1, p. 665. In another sense Barth would deny that all are in the body of Christ, since the reality of Christ's salvation is evident only to those who have faith.

28. *Ibid.*, IV, 3 b, p. 790.

29. Barth, *Theology and Church*, p. 348. Cf. *Church Dogmatics*, I, 1, p. 539.

30. *Church Dogmatics*, IV, 3 b, p. 931.

31. Robert S. Paul, *The Church in Search of Its Self* (Grand Rapids: Eerdmans, 1972), p. 367.

32. John Calvin, *Commentary on the Epistles of Paul the Apostle to the Corinthians*, Vol. I, trans. John Pringle (Edinburgh: T. Constable for Calvin Translating Society, 1848), p. 208.

33. Barth, *Church Dogmatics*, IV, 1, p. 76.

34. Berkouwer, *The Triumph of Grace in the Theology of Karl Barth*, p. 264.

35. Barth, *The Epistle to the Philippians*, p. 108.

36. Calvin, *Institutes of the Christian Religion*, III, 1, 1 (XX, 537).

37. Cf. his description of the "principalities and powers" in Karl Barth, *Community, Church and State* (Garden City, N.Y.: Doubleday, 1960), p. 50.

38. Barth is, of course, correct that evil has no ultimate ontological status, but I contend that it nevertheless has an ontological ground, viz., the transcendent freedom of man and the angels. It is finally to be traced to the divine permission that makes possible the impossible act of rebellion. It is both creative and destructive and should probably be described as anti-being even more than nonbeing. It is not simply a negation but a "positive negation" (Emil Brunner). It consists not so much in a turning away from the Real to the Unreal as in a desire to be God.

39. Barth, *Church Dogmatics*, II, 2, p. 170. (Italics mine.)

40. Barth, *Community, Church and State*, pp. 116, 117.

41. Barth, *Church Dogmatics*, III, 3, p. 362.

42. Barth has consistently argued for the demythologizing of demonology. In his later years he virtually gave up the concept of devils or demons. See Godsey, *Karl Barth's Table Talk*, pp. 72, 73.

43. Markus Barth, *The Broken Wall* (Philadelphia: Judson Press, 1959), p. 263. I maintain on the contrary that the cross of

Christ does not render the demonic powers harmless but that it secures the believer against them. The demonic powers, to be sure, have been dismantled (Col. 2:15), but this means not that they no longer possess destructive power but that their weapons have been rendered ineffectual against the power of faith.

44. Barth, *Church Dogmatics*, III, 3, p. 364.
45. He can even say that "the defeated enemy is still capable of attack in his dangerous death-throes." *Church Dogmatics*, IV, 3 a, p. 336. Yet the meaning here is that the devil is still capable of deception, since it has "only the force of a dangerous appearance."
46. Barth says that in Jesus Christ the "antithesis is met and overcome." *Church Dogmatics*, IV, 1, p. 35.
47. From his *Journals*. Quoted in Jacques Ellul, *Hope in Time of Abandonment*, trans. C. Edward Hopkin (New York: Seabury Press, 1973), p. 149.
48. Quoted in H. R. Mackintosh, *Types of Modern Theology*, 6th ed. (London: Nisbet & Co., 1949), p. 238.
49. Godsey, *Karl Barth's Table Talk*, p. 16.
50. Barth, *Church Dogmatics*, IV, 3 b, p. 869.
51. Barth makes clear that his conception of preaching "does not imply that the hearer is called to make a decision. A decision, if it is made, is a matter between the individual and God alone and is not a necessary element in preaching." In his *Preaching of the Gospel*, p. 10.
52. Barth writes: "God's action never takes place 'in and under.' It certainly takes place 'with' man's activity, but also above and in face of it." *Church Dogmatics*, III, 4, p. 521.
53. *Ibid.*, IV, 3 b, p. 852.
54. Barth, *The Epistle to the Romans*, 6th ed. trans., p. 38.
55. Godsey, *Karl Barth's Table Talk*, p. 87.
56. Karl Barth, *Deliverance to the Captives*, trans. Marguerite Wieser (London: SCM Press, 1959), p. 37.
57. Barth, *The Preaching of the Gospel*, p. 17.
58. *Ibid.*, p. 90.
59. Perhaps Kierkegaard erred slightly in the direction of subjectivism, but Barth would have been greatly aided had he continued to draw upon Kierkegaard. Arthur Cochrane has maintained that Barth needs to be corrected at times by Kierkegaard.

60. Emil Brunner, *The Christian Doctrine of God,* trans. Olive Wyon (Philadelphia: Westminster Press, 1950), p. 351.
61. Barth, *Church Dogmatics,* IV, 3 b, p. 873.
62. Scriptural passages worthy of special examination in this connection are Matt. 16:18; I Cor. 15:29; Eph. 4:8-10; I Pet. 3:19, 20; 4:6.
63. It is not my intention here to denigrate Arminianism, which in its original form is to be sharply distinguished from Pelagianism. Arminian motifs such as the ability to resist grace and to fall from grace are considerably qualified in Barth, who maintains that grace in the long run will triumph over man's resistance and that though we can defy grace we can never escape from it. Barth tends to transcend the traditional cleavage between Arminianism and Calvinism.
64. At the same time, Barth reopens the door to the doctrine of the secret will of God by allowing for the incomprehensible possibility of self-damnation even on the part of those who at one time in their lives were genuinely committed to Christ. Sometimes the impression is given that this self-damnation is tantamount to eternal condemnation, but as we have seen there is an ambiguity in Barth in this area of his theology.
65. Barth, *The Humanity of God,* p. 11.

172

Index of Names

Index of Subjects